WINES
OF
WALLA WALLA VALLEY

A DEEP-ROOTED HISTORY

CATIE McINTYRE WALKER
Foreword by Dr. Myles J. Anderson

AMERICAN PALATE

Published by American Palate
A Division of The History Press
Charleston, SC 29403
www.historypress.net

ISBN 978.1.62619.168.6

Library of Congress Control Number: 2014953173

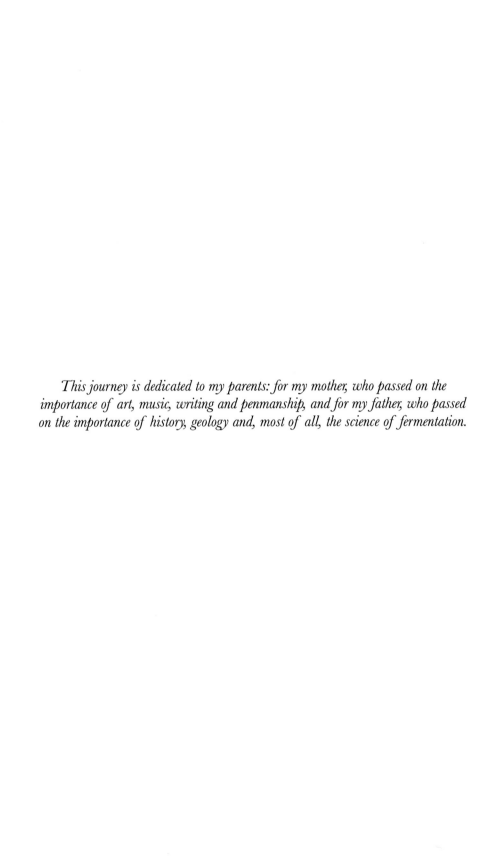

This journey is dedicated to my parents: for my mother, who passed on the importance of art, music, writing and penmanship, and for my father, who passed on the importance of history, geology and, most of all, the science of fermentation.

CONTENTS

FOREWORD

When my wife, Myrna, and I moved to Walla Walla in 1977, there was but one winery and one wine shop. Tasting rooms were unheard of. The downtown looked perhaps like a bomb had exploded as many of the businesses had closed or moved. The restaurant scene was grim. The recommended restaurant was the Pastime, a family-owned Italian café, which had recently shut its doors.

Leonetti Cellar, the first modern-day winery, changed Walla Walla's quality of life. Its 1978 Cabernet Sauvignon was chosen as the "Best Cabernet Sauvignon in America" by *The Wine and Spirits Guide*. This was the beginning of the development of Walla Walla as a bona fide wine destination. Wine enthusiasts nationwide wanted to buy and taste this wine. The Gallo brothers sent a private jet to Walla Walla to buy a case of the amazing wine and to meet Gary and Nancy Figgins.

Prior to 1977, most of the grape farming and winemaking was done as part of backyard gardens. The wine was homemade. Catie McIntyre Walker describes this scenario splendidly in *Wines of Walla Walla Valley: A Deep-Rooted History*.

Catie was a 2004 graduate of the Institute for Enology and Viticulture program at Walla Walla Community College. She soon began to write a blog titled "Through the Walla Walla Grape Vine." She founded the Wild Walla Walla Wine Woman, an online wine shop, which precipitated her opening a downtown wine shop by the same name. She has since returned to writing. Catie acquired her interest in writing about Northwest history from her father, who was a compulsive history buff.

Foreword

As a part of the modern wine scene, I was privileged to know most of the major players and witness the astonishing changes in the economic character of Walla Walla brought on by the wine industry. Catie captures all of this with this well-researched document. This is a delightful read for the wine enthusiast interested in Walla Walla, its winemakers, their wines and the wine community.

Pour a glass of wine, sit back and enjoy the wonderful history of the original settlers, creation of the terroir, modern-day winemakers, grape growers and supporting characters who are a part of the ever-developing Walla Walla wine scene. Voilà!

MYLES J. ANDERSON, EDD
Founding Director, Institute of Enology and Viticulture
Walla Walla

ACKNOWLEDGEMENTS

There is an old proverb that says, "It takes a whole village to raise a child," and it just so happens it takes a whole village to write a book about a village. This isn't my book. I just gathered up the facts, memories and photos and compiled them all together.

First of all, the acknowledgements begin with my family. Growing up, my dad would herd my siblings and me to the backseat of the car and take us for a ride on Sunday afternoons. Mom would pack a picnic lunch. We would visit various monuments and museums, as well as fields and riverbanks looking for treasures from fossils to agates. While other children spent their summer vacation at Disneyland, the McIntyre children begrudgingly spent their vacation at the Smithsonian. Thank you to my siblings, Terry, Connie and Caren, for putting up with my motion sickness on these childhood adventures, and to my parents, who understood the importance of our history, especially local history and geology.

The first two chapters of this book have been tucked away for several years, just waiting for the right time. Thank you to former commissioning editor at The History Press and the American Palate series Aubrie Koenig for finding me. Also, thanks to Alyssa Pierce, commissioning editor at The History Press, for inheriting me and assisting me with much patience on this project.

In this journey of writing about wine, special thanks go to Dr. Myles Anderson for being a mentor, contributing the foreword and believing I should write Volume 2. Thank you to friend Nick Velluzzi, for his interest in

ACKNOWLEDGEMENTS

Walla Walla, finding his way back to Walla Walla and for his contribution of the afterword; Kevin Pogue, professor of Geology at Whitman College, for making sure I had my facts correct about Walla Walla's fascinating geology; good friend Jeff Reynolds for backing me up on editing and indexing; journalist Steven P. Bjerklie for believing in me so many moons ago; and the late Stan Clarke, wine guru and former viticulture instructor who lectured me one day, "If you fail, I fail, and I am not going to fail." I will never forget those words.

Additional thanks to Duane Wollmuth, executive director, and Heather Bradshaw, communications and marketing manager, of the Walla Walla Valley Wine Alliance; James Payne, executive director, and his staff, Laura and Greg, at Fort Walla Walla Museum; Melissa Williams and Dave Walk from Walla Walla Community College for assisting me with the Institute of Viticulture and Enology photos; Joe Drazan of the Bygone Walla Walla Project for his photo research and enthusiasm about the project; and to many others who shared their photographs, stories and recipes—you will see their names throughout the book. Thank you, all.

INTRODUCTION

We have come full circle. There is an old biblical quote from Corinthians that states, "Grow where you're planted." We have indeed witnessed the growth of our valley, as well as our own personal growth.

It's an important story to tell. There are those of us who were fortunate enough to be born and raised in this valley, and we understand it like no other. Some of us have chosen to stay, and of those who leave, many will return. There are the newcomers who have chosen to make Walla Walla their home, and for those who are "home growns," sometimes we take our little valley for granted. It's then we need to look through the eyes of the newcomers, and even our visitors, and take the time to see what brought them here: a valley filled with rich history; magnificent architecture; a diverse, artistic and intellectual culture; a relaxed and friendly environment; four distinct seasons; blue and lavender shaded mountains; green and gold foothills; clean air and water; an abundance of agriculture; and, of course, the wine.

The many of us who have grown up where we were planted have seen the fame of our small city's name only spoofed in movies and cartoons, as Bing Crosby's (a Washington State's native son, actor and singer) character Hank Martin did in the 1949 movie *A Connecticut Yankee in King Arthur's Court*. Hank had to convince King Arthur he had magical power and created a long incantation of "magic" starting with "Walla Walla, Washington…"

In the comic strip *Pogo*, artist Walt Kelly wrote a well-known fractured yuletide carol, "Deck Us All with Boston Charlie, Walla Walla, Wash an' Kalamazoo!" And of course, there were the Chipmunks singing the "Witch

Doctor" with "Walla Walla Bing Bang." But one of the most memorable was Warner Brothers' 1953 cartoon of Bugs Bunny portraying a persistent door-to-door salesman for the fictional "Little Giant Vacuum Cleaner Company of Walla Walla, Washington."

However, it was 1960s popular comedian George Carlin's onstage act that came the closest to the real Walla Walla. In his act, Carlin would portray Willie West, a DJ for "Wonderful WINO Radio, located in Western Walla Walla." Did Carlin have a premonition?

Walla Walla has come a long way from the days of being spoofed by comics. Today, the valley is receiving awards and accolades not only for its wine and award-winning chefs and dining but also for friendliest town, its historical trees and downtown, top place to retire and top travel destination, to name a few.

Recently Kevin Pogue, professor of Geology at Whitman College in Walla Walla, pointed out to me a list of the highest "Classic-Scoring Wines of 2013" from a national wine magazine with a distribution around the world. Rated among the leaders of wine from France and California, several wines from Walla Walla were listed among the best with scores from 95 to 98 on a 100-point scale. Some of the local wines received higher scores than those of the Old World classics of France. In other words, Walla Walla wines are world class.

Unfortunately, not everyone in Walla Walla approves of the wine culture. Like anything, there will always be the critics. It has been my experience from their e-mails and messages to me that some critics view wine drinkers as "alcoholics." A true lover of wine understands that an excessive amount of alcohol in wine can create a wine out of balance and defeat the purpose of what the winemaker strives for—the nuances of wine, the differences of aromas and flavors between grapes that were grown north of Walla Walla in former wheat land versus grapes that were grown south of the city in rocky river beds in the former channels of the Walla Walla River. Besides, alcoholics typically do not purchase high-end award-winning wines and take the bottles home to age for a few years in their cellars. The critics, hoping for a popular chain restaurant or store, complain when a new winery moves to downtown. Landlords cannot afford to turn away a business ready to invest in their property, let alone investing in our community. The critics accuse the "city fathers" of pandering solely to the wineries, especially downtown, and yet the majority of the wineries are not even located in the city limits but in Walla Walla County. The critics complain when there are potholes, malls and swimming pools in need of replacement or repair with expectations that the wineries should pay the bills. Yet, the same critics never expected that of the wheat farmers who make up the majority of the agricultural businesses in our valley. The critics complain that the presence of the wineries creates an unsavory environment for children by promoting alcohol. If anything, we hope that the presence of wineries creates knowledge and respect about alcohol, along with, first and foremost, parental guidance.

Change is difficult for all of us. However, I believe to keep and preserve the things that we cherish, sometimes changes must be made. It's been said by the critics of the wine culture, "We want *it* (Walla Walla) back to the way it used to be." I often ask the critic, "Which decade or century?"

From the Stone Age to Ancient Greece, fermented beverages, such as beer and wine, have been produced by humans. At the time, alcoholic beverages provided nutrition, a trading commodity, medication and a social outlet accompanied with food and also played a role in religion—and the same has been recorded in Walla Walla's own history. The United State's third president, Thomas Jefferson, was known as America's first wine connoisseur and had a major vision and influence on America's part in the world's wine stage even before the northwestern territory of Washington was granted statehood in 1889.

In the 1800s, the French and Italian settlers brought to the Walla Walla Valley their European culture of wine and their knowledge of wine grape growing and winemaking that had been handed down through the generations; and the German-born settlers to Walla Walla brought with them the knowledge of brewing beer (another story altogether). Walla Walla was the largest town in Washington in the 1860s and 1870s and would flourish with the arrival of gold miners from the neighboring state of Idaho. Soon there would be over thirty taverns and liquor stores downtown, and the town would continue to grow in population and businesses through the early 1900s. Wineries, breweries, taverns and liquor stores would continue to grow in Walla Walla until Prohibition.

Walla Walla was no different from any other town during the era of the late 1860 to the 1900s, as the mayor of Walla Walla and his five councilmen noticed that of all the new businesses, the saloons were the most active and their revenue most essential to the life of their new town of Walla Walla.

The Walla Walla I remember growing up in was a vibrant downtown filled with specialty shops, fine clothing boutiques for men and women, several high-end shoe shops, a fur shop and storage, a shoe-shining shop, a French hat shop, department stores, theaters, cafés and coffee shops, as well as several cigar stores, taverns and billiard halls. The latter three businesses I was not supposed to know about, but I knew of their existence.

INTRODUCTION

As a child, going to town with my maternal grandmother on a summer afternoon was an event. She would change from one of her "house" dresses to one she wore to her club luncheons or church, and sometimes, she would even wear a hat. On a Friday afternoon, I can remember my father phoning my mother from work to "get the kids ready," which meant as soon as he came home from work, we were going downtown for dinner and some window shopping. The downtown I remember growing up in was a vibrant community.

Along came the 1970s, and by the end of that decade and during the 1980s, downtown Walla Walla had lost its charm and appeal. The caretakers of the old shops had either retired or died, leaving families to either change their business models or, for most, simply close the doors. The malls arrived and offered the department store amenities shoppers could not get downtown, including more retail space on one convenient level, constant seventy-two-degree temperatures and free parking.

The town of Walla Walla was lined with buildings sporting the outdated store façades of the '50s and '60s, with a vacancy rate of almost 30 percent. What buildings were occupied, ironically, were banks, investment companies and real estate offices. The jewel of the city, the historic Marcus Whitman Hotel, had declined. Visitors to the city would later describe downtown by painting a scene of a western ghost town with one dried, lone tumbleweed traveling down dusty roads.

The year 1984 was a year of progress as the Walla Walla Main Street Foundation (eventually renamed the Downtown Foundation) was formed by concerned businesses and property owners, and the Walla Walla Valley was officially designated an American Viticultural Area (AVA) with only four bonded wineries. In 1999, the Marcus Whitman hotel was restored to its classic elegance and detail and officially reopened in 2001. The rest, as they say, is history but also a sign of a promising future.

Today, Walla Walla illuminates a vibrant downtown with its old historic buildings filled with specialty shops, fine clothing boutiques, a live theater, many music venues, spas, galleries, bakeries, restaurants, cafés, coffee shops and several winery tasting rooms, as well as a seasonal farmers' market and various annual street festivals. It is this decade—in fact, it is in this new century—in which Walla Walla is back to the way it "used to be."

The livelihoods of the wineries have brought in a whole new industry: tourism. Once again the critics speak while not understanding the tourist industry affects us all through revenue taxes and employment. Tourism and the wine industry provide jobs, and not just jobs at wineries, restaurants and lodging facilities, but throughout many unrelated industries, as well. The over one hundred wineries need services from contractors, plumbers, electricians, landscapers, food service professionals and technicians. Today's tourists are no different than the Idaho miners and settlers who the former merchants of the "Old West" Walla Walla romanced and depended on for the town's growth and livelihood.

The wineries of the Walla Walla Valley, no matter how large or small, are on what I refer to as my list of unsung heroes. Here I include all the people who make substantive, yet often unrecognized contributions but who are seldom acknowledged. There is rarely a day that goes by when wineries are not asked to donate to a charitable cause, no matter for a large nonprofit or a very private donation to assist a local person with his or her medical bills. One cannot attend a fundraiser in the Walla Walla Valley where there isn't a bottle of local wine that is being auctioned off. Unfortunately there are people who assume that owning a winery automatically means a luxurious lifestyle, but for the most part, at least in Walla Walla, owning a winery is no different than owning any small mom-and-pop business or small farm.

In March 2014, the *Walla Walla Union-Bulletin* newspaper reported in an editorial that between donated auction lots and personal donations from the wineries of Walla Walla, the local wineries raised $299,518 for Seattle Children's Hospital at the annual 2013 Auction of Washington Wines with a grand total of $2 million collectively from wineries across the state of Washington. The nearly $300,000 raised by our Walla Walla wineries comes close to the $325,000 in uncompensated care provided for 238 young patients from Walla Walla County at the Seattle Children's Hospital as well many other children from the Walla Walla Valley who received medical care at the Seattle Children's Tri-Cities Clinic, located in Richland, sixty miles away from Walla Walla.

Throughout the journey of this book you will read a story of how history repeats itself. As you turn the pages, the history of the pioneers who brought the wine culture to our valley will unfold, as will the stories of the new pioneers and the visionaries. Much of our rich history has evolved in the valley's wines, and many of the wineries give tribute to the historic places and pioneers of the Walla Walla Valley.

Our European settlers, especially those from France and Italy, left a culture behind in the Old World where wine was considered food. Wine was served with most meals and was almost as important as the loaf of bread on the table. With our settlers' rich history in agriculture—as well as accolades for our award-winning chefs, James Beard Foundation dinners and other national press and awards regarding our fine dining and use of local foods—therefore it only made sense to include favorite recipes from some of the wineries and local chefs.

If you are so inclined, relax with a glass of wine and explore the deep-rooted history about the wines from the Walla Walla Valley. There were only so many pages allowed to create this book, yet still so many stories and wineries to share. Even though not all the wineries' stories were told, I can guarantee you that every winery in our valley is very special, and each one is worth visiting. Perhaps someday, there will be another book.

Happy thirtieth anniversary to the Walla Walla Valley Wine Alliance.

The thirtieth anniversary logo of the Walla Walla Valley wine region. *Courtesy of Walla Walla Wine Alliance.*

1

WELTER AND WASTE

In the beginning God created the heavens and the earth. And the earth then was welter and waste and darkness over the deep and a powerful wind hovering over the waters, and God said, "Let there be light," and there was light...[and] dry land and seas and plants and trees which grew fruit with seed.
—Book of Genesis

The highly diverse geology of Washington State is proof there was "welter and waste and darkness over the deep and a powerful wind was hovering over the waters." This state, located in the Northwest, has been the stage for intrusions of igneous and metamorphic rocks, volcanic activity, mountain-building episodes, erosion and massive flooding events. Today, the wind still hovers over the majestic waters of the Columbia River just above Wallula Gap in Walla Walla County in the southeastern part of the state.

Throughout the dry land of the state, there are indeed trees growing "fruit with seed," the same forbidden fruit with origins in the Garden of Eden, and today producing over 60 percent of the nation's apples. In the Book of Genesis a patriarch named Noah, the tiller of the soil, was the first man to have planted a vineyard bearing clusters of "fruit with seed." Vineyards were also planted in the state of Washington as early as 1825 and have been planted since, with over forty-four thousand acres as of 2011.

Over ten million years ago, a vast area that is now known as the Columbia Basin, located in eastern Washington, was engulfed with one of the largest basaltic lava floods ever to appear on the earth, covering sixty-three thousand square miles of the Pacific Northwest. The hot and angry lava flowed, reaching a thickness of more than twelve thousand feet. The molten rock erupted as the crust of the earth subsided, creating a broad, depressed lava plain.

Most of the flows were extruded near the southeast corner of the state east of Walla Walla County. Many of these fluid trails of lava traveled as far as the Pacific Ocean, guided by the ancestral Columbia River drainage. The hardened lava flows were eventually sculpted by erosion, stones were deposited, lakebeds and natural dams were formed and forests grew.

In the southeast corner of Washington and the northeastern part of Oregon, 4,060 square miles of a broad uplift of basalt lava created a subprovince of the Columbia Basin, known as the Blue Mountains. The highest peak of the mountain range is 9,108 feet. Today the Blue Mountains are drained by several rivers, including the Grande Ronde and Tucannon, tributaries of the Snake River, as well as the forks of the John Day, Umatilla and Walla Walla Rivers, which are tributaries of the great Columbia.

In time, the lava cooled and solidified into basalt throughout the Columbia Basin, including the area of the Walla Walla River. Then, the floods came.

Thousands of years later, expeditions and early settlers traveling from the east of the continent would take note that the rugged and severely eroded landscapes in eastern Washington were quite unusual and different from any other land they had seen. The cataclysmic series of floods—named after Lake Missoula and also known as the Spokane Floods or Bretz Floods (named after geologist J. Harlen Bretz, who first recognized evidence of these catastrophic floods and referred to them as the Spokane Floods in the 1920s)—left behind proof that an ice age had occurred.

These violent natural floods, which caused great upheaval, destruction and fundamental change to significant ways of life in the region, took place during the last ice age over twelve thousand years ago.

The glacial prehistoric Lake Missoula, located in what is now the western state of Montana, was originally a body of water that was as large as half the size of Lake Michigan. Lake Missoula measured about three thousand square miles and contained five cubic miles of water. The sequences of floods occurred about forty times during a two-thousand-year period and swept like tsunamis across Washington and Idaho. The speed of the floods reached sixty-two miles per hour, and the great glacial lake of Missoula would be drained in periods as short as two days.

These series of violent, yet natural outbursts of water were constricted as they passed through an uplifted ridge of basalt, at a point now known as the Wallula Gap, just south of the confluence of the Walla Walla and Columbia

Rivers. The constricted water slowed and backed up into the valleys of the Yakima and Walla Walla Rivers, leaving behind layers of sediment. Today, these rhythmic beds are known as the Touchet Beds because of their exposures in cliffs along the Walla Walla River near the hamlet of Touchet.

Powerful southwest winds carried the flood-deposited silt from the barren tracts of land and up to the northeast areas of eastern Washington and northern Idaho and left behind layers of loess. The angular grains of the wind-blown dust would eventually develop into the rich soil of the loess deposits in the fertile agriculture regions.

These soils and unique landscapes that were formed and left behind by cataclysmic events would eventually define the agriculture that would be grown in this region, and it turns out, they would be especially good at growing "the fruit with seed."

2

PLACE OF MANY WATERS

Eventually, all things merge into one, and a river runs through it. The river was cut by the world's great flood and runs over rocks from the basement of time. On some of the rocks are timeless raindrops. Under the rocks are the words, and some of the words are theirs. I am haunted by waters.
Norman Maclean, A River Runs Through It and Other Stories

Walla Walla County is tucked away in the southeastern corner of Washington State. On April 25, 1854, the Washington Territorial Assembly created the 1,299-square-mile county, and this fertile valley was one of the first areas in the region between the Rockies and the Cascades to be permanently settled.

On November 11, 1875, Columbia County, east of Walla Walla, was established, forming Walla Walla County's eastern border and the present-day Walla Walla County boundary line (1,267 square miles). The southern border is the state of Oregon, the eastern border is the state of Idaho and the Snake River separates the western and northern border from Washington's Benton and Franklin Counties. As of the 2010 census, the population of Walla Walla County was 58,781.

The population of Walla Walla was developed around the U.S. military's Fort Walla Walla in the late 1850s, and the city of Walla Walla was granted a municipal charter in January 1862. It is the largest city in the county, as well as the county seat, and the twenty-fourth-largest city in Washington. Today, the population within the city limits is 31,731.

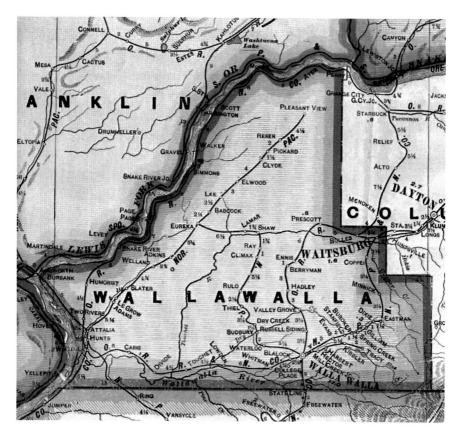

Walla Walla County map, 1909. *Courtesy of Census Finder Records.*

The true natives of this northwest country of the new Americas were the Sahaptin people, a hunter-gatherer society that had inhabited land on the Columbia River Plateau for centuries. This land, which was engraved by lava many centuries before, was located in the northeastern part of Oregon and southeastern part of Washington State. Those tribes of the Sahaptin people included the Nez Perce, Cayuse, Umatilla, Yakama (Yakima) and Walla Walla.

The name Walla Walla, loosely translated from Wallulapum, the native language of the Walla Walla people, meant "many waters."

Historians and the U.S. Geological Survey claim there are more than twenty different spellings of "Walla Walla" in early journals and maps. Some of the varied spellings come from the early natives, the Walla Walla Native American tribe, and Meriwether Lewis and William Clark of the Lewis and Clark expedition. Lewis and Clark referred to the Walla Walla

River as Wolloh Wolloh, and Clark spelled the name Wallah Wallah in one of his journal entries. Other names and spellings included Wallow Wallows, Wollah Wollah, Wollaw Wollah and Woller Woller, to name a few.

In 1843, Captain John C. Frémont, an American military officer, explorer and politician who became the first candidate of the antislavery Republican Party for the office of president, called the river "Walahwalah" during an expedition on the Oregon Trail and into the Sierra Nevadas, led by his guide, Kit Carson:

> *The weather was pleasant, with a sunrise temperature of 36°. Our road to-day had in it nothing of interest; and the country offered to the eye only a sandy, undulating plain, through which a scantily timbered river takes its course. We halted about three miles above the mouth, on account of grass; and the next morning arrived at the Nez Perce fort, one of the trading establishments of the Hudson Bay Company, a few hundred yards above the junction of the Walahwalah with the Columbia river. Here we had the first view of this river, and found it about 1,200 yards wide, and presenting the appearance of a fine navigable stream.*

There are other historians who claim the name Walla Walla is from a Nez Perce and Cayuse word, *walatsa*, which means "running." This name was probably used in reference to the running waters of the Walla Walla River. Walla Walla has also been interpreted as the "place of many waters," referring to its many tributaries.

Poets had their own versions of where this green valley received its name. Joaquin Miller—the pen name of the colorful American poet Cincinnatus Heine (or Hiner) Miller (1837–1913), also nicknamed the "Poet of the Sierras" and the "Byron of the Rockies"—insisted that when the French voyagers first looked down from the Les Montagnes Bleues (the Blue Mountains) into this fair fertile valley they exclaimed, "Voilà Yoila!"

Questions were raised if the poem "Evangeline" by Henry Wadsworth Longfellow mentions "Walleway" as the poetical name of Walla Walla:

> *Far in the West there lies a desert land where mountains*
> *Lift through perpetual snows their lofty and luminous summits*
> *Down from their jagged deep ravines where the gorge like a gateway*
> *Opens a passing rude to the wheels of the emigrant's wagon*
> *Westward the Oregon flows and the Walleway and Owyhee.*

The final word regarding the name of Walla Walla is from the locals who live and work in this valley, and they will tell you Walla Walla is "the city so nice, they named it twice!" Local legend is that vaudeville performer Al Jolson coined the phrase when he performed at the Keylor Grand Theater, built in 1905 in downtown Walla Walla.

This lush fertile valley that was so nice and named twice is circled almost completely with rugged rocks of basalt and is indeed a place of "many waters." The Snake River, the largest tributary of the majestic Columbia River, marks the western and northern border of Walla Walla. The Columbia River, the largest North American river, forges a path bordering the two states of Washington and Oregon and eventually empties into the Pacific Ocean.

The Walla Walla River begins its route in the Blue Mountains on the Oregon side in Umatilla County, flows into Walla Walla County and continues to run fifty miles into the Columbia River just above the Wallula Gap. Its largest tributary, the Touchet River, takes its beginnings outside the Walla Walla County line. Other tributaries within the county line of Walla Walla include Mill Creek, Pine Creek and Dry Creek. The low, flat land along the Walla Walla and Touchet Rivers has been proven to be exceptionally fertile.

Mill Creek flows into Oregon and then back into Washington, joining the Walla Walla River. The creek splits into several branches at the eastern end of the city of Walla Walla and travels six miles through the city, including downtown. In 1948, Mill Creek was modified by the U.S. Army Corps of Engineers to control flooding.

The distributaries of Mill Creek include Blue Creek, Coppei Creek and Yellowhawk Creek. Other dominant creeks in the Walla Walla Valley include Russell Creek, Cottonwood Creek and Garrison Creek, to name a few.

Bennington Lake is the only public and recreational lake located in the Walla Walla Valley. This off-stream reservoir covers about fifty-two surface acres and is filled to a recreational pool of elevation 1,205 feet above sea level in the spring once the risk of flooding from Mill Creek is low.

The Walla Walla River would not only play a vital part for the area's water supply but also be an important focus for the fur traders who settled in the area after the Lewis and Clark expedition in 1804–06. The Canadian North West Fur Company and the Pacific Fur Company (originally owned by American businessman John Jacob Astor and eventually purchased by the British) settled in the area and were later followed by the Hudson's Bay Company. In 1818, the North West Fur Company built Fort Walla Walla. It

This engraving of a Nez Perce camp outside the walls of Old Fort Walla Walla on the Columbia River was made in 1853. *Courtesy of University of Washington Libraries.*

was originally established as Fort Nez Perce and was the first trading post in the area. It was built with permission of the Walla Walla tribal leader Chief Tamatappam. Its location was about a half mile from the mouth of the Walla Walla River at the east bank of the grand Columbia River upstream from Wallula Gap. The Walla Walla River was vital to the building of the fort as it was used to float the building's timber one hundred miles. It would be one of the first three Fort Walla Wallas to be built.

Many of the French workmen of the Hudson's Bay Company married the women from the local tribes. They settled into the valley, built cabins, established farms and raised families around 1823. The area was named "Frenchtown," and a collection of French Canadian log cabins were built and strewn among the Indian camps west of the present-day hamlet of Lowden. Frenchtown's "Main Street" was the Walla Walla River.

Irrigation was essential to this green valley of family gardens, orchards and crops. In 1836, physician and missionary Dr. Marcus Whitman was known to have dug the first irrigation ditch near his home in Walla Walla in addition to bringing strawberry and grapes vines and apple and vegetable seeds to the low, fertile land around the Walla Walla River. Other early settlers followed his practice of irrigation ditches, including two large-scale projects that were later launched in 1892–93 and known as the Burlingame-Gardena Ditch and the Hawley Ditch. These new irrigation methods would eventually transform thousands of dry acres into green farmland and bountiful orchards, especially apple orchards, throughout the Walla Walla Valley.

Whitman and his wife, Narcissa Prentiss Whitman, led the first party of wagon trains along the Oregon Trail, and together they established a mission at a Cayuse settlement at Waiilatpu (meaning "place of rye grass") located west of the northern end of the Blue Mountains, now six miles from the present-day city of Walla Walla. Dr. Whitman encouraged the neighboring native tribes to "settle down into an agricultural people." Farming was first met with contention, but eventually the early Americans understood there was a wealth of water for all, especially when each year, Whitman would lengthen the ditches and produce larger and more successful gardens.

Eventually flood irrigation proved to be successful around the bottomlands of the Walla Walla Valley, especially since they were flat. This type of irrigation also had the advantage of leaching out the salts in alkaline and saline soils.

In 1841, the U.S. Exploring Expedition, led by Lieutenant Charles Wilkes, visited the mission, observed the ditches and acknowledged that the area of Walla Walla was uncommonly "susceptible to irrigation" and that "a natural irrigation seems to take place" in the bottomlands, "owing to the numerous bends of the small streams, which almost convert a portion of the land into islands."

Other settlers who followed Whitman would soon discover that this little valley in eastern Washington, surrounded by the Blue Mountains, had all of the key elements for a cornucopia of agriculture. Wind-deposited silt, also known as "loess," provided exceptional drainage. A long growing season of an average two hundred days provided a summer of long hot days and cool nights and, with an additional two hours more sunlight per day, even compared to that in the more southern state of California.

It would be almost an ideal setting but lacked the desired rainfall with a high average of 20.86 inches in comparison to that of its western counterpart with an annual average of 34.10. However, what it lacked in rainfall, the rich valley made up for in the abundant water flow that surrounded it from the nearby snowfields collected at the neighboring blue-colored mountains, as W.D. Lyman describes in *Lyman's History of Old Walla Walla County*:

> One of the most interesting and important features of Walla Walla is the fine system of spouting artesian wells. There are now over thirty of these wells in the Walla Walla Valley, the largest having a flow of twenty-five hundred gallons per minute, sufficient to irrigate a half-section of land.

PLACE OF MANY WATERS

Owing to the immense snowfall in the Blue Mountains, ranging from ten to fifty or sixty feet during the season, a large part of the slopes and valleys below seems to be sub-irrigated and also to be underlaid by a great sheet of water.

In 1907, the farmers of the Walla Walla Valley acknowledged these wells and recognized their use as a new irrigation source. The artesian wells were a water source that seemed to defy gravity due to pressure building up between layers of rock. When the pressure was finally relieved with a path to the open air, it would gush, a natural fountain. This pure water was naturally filtered due to the porous rock it passed through on its journey to the top of the earth.

Grain crops, such as winter and spring wheat, barley and oats, were the most prolific in the higher elevation surrounding the valley, which required little to no irrigation, and by the late 1890s, wheat was Walla Walla's leading crop. Today, wheat has remained the leading and largest crop in the Walla Walla Valley with an average of 300,000 acres.

The first nursery in Walla Walla was staked out around 1859–61, and apple orchards and vineyards were planted by the creek banks of the Yellowhawk and Cottonwood, continuing into the border at Oregon. By the 1920s, the fruit orchard industry in the Walla Walla Valley had peaked. According to Lyman, "The most productive and compact single body of country is that portion of the Walla Walla Valley south of the state line extending to Milton, Ore."

It was noted by Lyman that not only orchards but also gardens were prolific in the area around the city of Walla Walla. Large and bountiful gardens and orchards in the valley were producing alfalfa, apples, asparagus, cherries, corn, onions, radishes, rhubarb, strawberries and extraordinarily large melons and squash. Walla Walla would be known for years as the "Garden City."

The 1870s brought new growth to the Walla Walla area with the extensive immigration of Italians. There were opportunities for settlers to mine for gold, to purchase land and to engage in farming—especially what was referred to as "truck gardens"—these small row crops of produce, such as onions, lettuce and carrots, were carted in trucks and sold at local markets.

A French soldier by the name of Peter Pieri was stationed on the Island of Corsica. Upon his discharge from the French army, he secured an Italian seed that was common on the island. In the early 1900s, Pieri settled in the Walla Walla Valley and planted the seed of the "French" onion on his

Bird's-eye view of Walla Walla, Washington Territory, in 1876, by cartographer E.S. Glover. *Courtesy of University of Washington Libraries.*

irrigated patch of land. Soon, his Italian immigrant neighbors noticed the exceptionally mild, sweet flavor of the onion, and by 1920, Pieri's neighbors adopted the sweet globe. Due to the low sulfur content and plenty of Walla Walla water, the famous Walla Walla Sweet Onion was born. Today, third and fourth generations of farmers still grow this crispy, sweet bulb.

The Italians made their livings not only from truck gardens and onions but also from vineyards in the valley, which they grew for both commercial and personal use.

The art of irrigation grew in the Walla Walla Valley, and by 1978, there were over 80,000 acres under some form of irrigation. Eventually, sprinklers from wheel lines were used, and today, drip line irrigation is now the dominant practice throughout the vineyards. As growth moved forward through the years, many of the old ditch companies consolidated into the Walla Walla River Irrigation District (WWRID). This district currently holds the legacy of the oldest water rights in the neighboring state of Oregon with some dating back to the late 1860s. The Walla Walla River Irrigation District today serves about 3,500 acres. The primary crops include apples, cherries, prunes and the world-class Walla Walla Valley wine grapes.

However, the prosperity of irrigation could not be accomplished without the area's resource management and environment. In the beginning of the twenty-first century, the U.S. Fish and Wildlife Service

WALLA WALLA SWEET ONION JAM

2 pounds Walla Walla Sweet Onions
6 tablespoons mild olive oil
2 tablespoons brown sugar, packed
pinch kosher salt
4 tablespoons balsamic vinegar

Slice onions ¼ inch thick and dice. Heat olive oil in a pan and sauté onions for 8 to 10 minutes. Add sugar, salt and balsamic vinegar. Continue to cook until the mixture turns thick and a deep golden brown. Serve hot or room temperature as a condiment over salmon or beef.

Recipe courtesy of Chef Caren McIntyre, graduate of Walla Walla Community College Culinary Arts Institute and lead pastry chef for Bon Appetit at Whitman College.

sent notice to the three main Walla Walla Valley irrigators: Walla Walla River Irrigation District, Hudson Bay District Improvement Company and Gardena North 2800 (until 2012, it was Gardena Farms Irrigation District No. 13). It had been suggested these districts were in violation of the Endangered Species Act of 1973 due to bringing levels of the Walla Walla River so low that bull trout and steelhead could possibly be harmed. A decade later, many former open canals were converted to pipelines making the conveyance of water more efficient by leaving more water in the river for the native fish.

The water and the local environment has continued to be protected by various agencies, including the Walla Walla Basin Watershed Council, which fosters education and cooperation to improve and maintain a healthy watershed for fish, invertebrates, plants and people of the Walla Walla Valley and Umatilla County, Oregon.

With the growth of the wineries and commercial vineyards, a voluntary group of winegrowers formed the Vinea Trust. It follows the guidelines of other environmental agencies, such as LIVE (Low-Input Viticulture Enology of the Pacific Northwest), IOBC (International Organization for Biological and Integrated Control) and Salmon-Safe (dedicated to restoring and maintaining healthy watersheds). These stewards of the land and vines have embraced a covenant of sustainable vineyard management that is synonymous with the Walla Walla Valley, recognizing strict environmental standards as well as high-quality farming practices.

WALLA WALLA PICKLED ASPARAGUS

20 pounds fresh asparagus spears
7 to 10 quart-sized pickling jars with lids and rings
4 to 5 garlic bulbs, cloves peeled
6 fresh jalapeño peppers, sliced into rings
fresh dill
7 cups boiling water
2½ cups sugar
7 teaspoons salt
2 teaspoons black pepper
7 cups white vinegar, for pickling

Wash asparagus well. Trim the bottoms of the spears according to the length of the jars being used. (It is recommended to use quart jars instead of pint jars to eliminate waste of asparagus spears). Wash and rinse canning jars; keep hot until ready to use. Prepare lids according to manufacturer's directions.

Into each jar, place a few cloves of garlic, a few jalapeño rings and a sprig of fresh dill prior to packing asparagus into jars. Combine boiling water, sugar, salt, pepper and vinegar to prepare pickling solution. (It is suggested to have extra ingredients for the hot pickling solution, as the original recipe never seems to be enough.)

Blanch the clean and trimmed asparagus in a boiling water bath for 2 minutes. Cool quickly in an ice bath. Drain. Pack into quart jars. Cover with hot pickling solution leaving ½-inch headspace. Remove air bubbles and adjust headspace, if needed. Wipe rims of jars with a dampened, clean paper towel; apply two-piece metal canning lids (lids and rings). Process jars in a canner pot with a boiling water bath for 10 minutes.

Recipe courtesy of Lori and Tim Kennedy of Don Carlo Vineyard

---

CORNMEAL QUICK BREAD WITH LEMON AND THYME

SERVES 4–6

¾ cup unsalted butter, softened, plus more for pan

⅓ cup all-purpose flour, plus more for pan

¾ cup sugar

1 tablespoon finely grated lemon zest

3 large eggs

2 tablespoons fresh lemon juice

1 tablespoon coarsely chopped fresh thyme leaves, plus sprig for garnish

1 cup fine yellow cornmeal

1 teaspoon baking powder

¾ teaspoon coarse salt

¼ cup pine nuts, toasted, half coarsely chopped and half whole

Preheat oven to 325 degrees. Butter a 9- by 5-inch loaf pan. Dust with flour and tap out excess; set aside. Put butter and sugar into a large bowl. With an electric mixer, beat on medium-high speed until pale and fluffy, about 3 minutes.

Add lemon zest; mix 1 minute. Add eggs, one at a time, mixing well after each addition. Mix in lemon juice and thyme. Add ⅓ cup flour, cornmeal, baking powder and salt, and mix until just combined. Stir in chopped pine nuts.

Pour batter into prepared pan. Sprinkle the top with whole pine nuts. Bake until a cake tester inserted into the center comes out clean, 50 to 55 minutes. Let cool completely on a wire rack. Garnish with thyme. Bread can be stored in an airtight container at room temperature for up to 2 days.

Recommended wine pairing: Dunham Cellars Shirley Mays Chardonnay.

Recipe courtesy of Joanne Dunham, Owner of Dunham Cellars.

3

PIONEERS OF THE GRAPE

The cultivation of the grape in this country is no longer an experiment. Indeed,
the success is so great that the more sanguine claim that our climate is as favorable
to the growth of the grape as that of California. This being the case, our grape
growers are already considering the question: Whence can they find a market for
the surplus crop?
—Walla Walla Statesman, *1876.*

America's founding father and third president, Thomas Jefferson, has
been described as America's "first distinguished viticulturist" and "the
greatest patron of wine and wine growing that this country has yet had."

While Jefferson may have commissioned the Lewis and Clark expedition
to explore the Northwest Territory, there was very little influence of
Jefferson's love of the grape in the great Wild West of Washington.
The early fur trappers of the Hudson's Bay Company, North West Fur
Company and the Pacific Fur Company, many of French descent, had
traditions of partaking in spirits and wine. The exchange of their pelts for
spirits from the distillery at Fort Vancouver, located near the Columbia
River, was common, but there was little wine to be found, though grapes
would later be planted at the fort.

Narcissa Prentiss Whitman, wife of Dr. Marcus Whitman, became one
of the most famous women of the West as she crossed the vast continent
from her first home of Prattsburg, New York, to what would be her last
home in Walla Walla. In her journals, as well as letters to her mother, she
would write about the hardships of the dusty and hot oppressive weather,

the endless dreary diets of dried meat and her dreams of bread, fresh fruits and vegetables.

Narcissa's dreams came true once she arrived at Fort Vancouver, Washington, which she referred to as the "New York of the Pacific Ocean." Fort Vancouver would be a stop for the Whitmans to rest and recollect before their difficult journey through the passage of the Blue Mountains to their final destination at the Walla Walla River, home of the Nez Perce and Cayuse tribes.

Washington State's first wine grapes, European *Vitis vinifera*, were eventually planted at Fort Vancouver by the Hudson's Bay Company in 1825, and it was at Fort Vancouver where Narcissa became enamored of the large prosperous gardens and where she dined on "fruits of every description and vegetables too numerous to mention." The knowledge and skills of irrigation that her husband, Dr. Whitman, brought with him from the fort proved valuable to their final settlement. Narcissa spoke of the seeds she would save and bring with her to the "place of many waters": "The grapes are just ripe, and I am feasting on them finely. There is now a bunch on the table before me. I save all the seeds of those I eat, for planting, & of apples. Also I intend taking some young sprouts of apple, peach, grape & strawberry vines & from the nursery here."

Mrs. Whitman wrote in a letter to her mother about her and Dr. Whitman dining with Dr. Jean-Baptiste "John" McLoughlin, the chief factor of Hudson's Bay Company at Fort Vancouver; officers; and other guests at the fort. The dinners were served European style, and with each course, there was an exchange of a clean plate. It was not a dining experience she had been used to in her travels, especially after being in a covered wagon for months. She described to her mother their main courses and that there were plates of grapes, cheese and bread or biscuits and that butter was produced to complete and round out the whole meal. However, there was one custom placed on the table she would not partake in: "There is one article on the table I have not yet mentioned & of which I never partake; that is wine. The gentlemen frequently drink toasts to each other but never give us the opportunity of refusing, for they know we are members of the teetotal society. We have many talks about drinking wine, but no one joins our society."

Dr. Marcus Whitman and his wife, Narcissa, eventually established the Whitman Mission in 1836 near the Walla Walla River. It was a day's ride from Fort Nez Perce at the east bank of the Columbia River and six miles to the east, which is now the city of Walla Walla.

Le Boucher Saloon and Barber Shop, 117 West Main Street, 1885. "Clem Bergevin" has been listed on the photo. Bergevin is an old family name with Frenchtown connections. *Courtesy of Joe Drazan, the Bygone Walla Walla Project.*

E. LE BOUCHER,

WINES AND LIQUORS,

THE FINEST IN THE CITY.

FOURTH AND MAIN.   OPP. STINE HOUSE.

Calling card for E. Le Boucher Wines and Liquors, "The Finest in the City." *Courtesy of Joe Drazan, the Bygone Walla Walla Project.*

The route to the mission would serve as an important way station for migrants on the Oregon Trail. Dr. Whitman farmed and provided medical care, and his wife set up a school for the children of the local tribes. On November 29, 1847, Dr. Whitman and Narcissa, along with eleven other settlers, perished in an attack by the Cayuse and Umatilla tribes. They accused Dr. Whitman of being unable to halt the spread of measles when two hundred members of the Cayuse people, who were in his medical care, died. Today, the incident remains controversial: to some, the Whitmans were pioneer heroes, but others saw them as white settlers who imposed their religion and spread illness. The Whitman massacre would be the start of what was known as the Cayuse War.

After the Whitman massacre in 1847, most of eastern Washington was closed off to settlement during the various wars with the neighboring tribes. In 1859, treaty negotiations were established and the area was finally reopened; however, in the meantime, new settlements had been channeled farther west to the Puget Sound area and north to the Willamette Valley in Oregon.

Around this time, gold mining was coming alive all through the continent, and the neighboring state of Idaho began to play a significant role in the economy of the southeastern area of Washington Territory. In 1860, the discovery of gold in northern Idaho created an inundation of settlers to the area that would last for over ten years as new mines were opened and claimed. Walla Walla saw opportunity and would contribute to this potential and exciting new economy by opening new businesses that would solicit to the prospectors and other settlers in the area. Walla Walla was to mining in Washington what Sacramento was to the gold rush in California.

The small town's Main Street in eastern Washington would become the highlight of the busiest town in Washington Territory. Shopkeepers would brag that their village had a larger population than any other town located on the Puget Sound. This was true, as Seattle did not reach its boom until the late 1800s.

During the growth of Walla Walla, Main Street and other nearby streets were lined with restaurants, grocers, butcher shops, furniture and hardware stores, drugstores, banks, bakeries, breweries, poultry markets, general mercantile stores, hotels, barbershops, candy stores, sewing machine shops, jewelry stores, dressmakers and tailor shops.

There were book and stationery stores, laundries, liveries, saddle makers and blacksmiths, liquor stores, cigar and tobacco shops and theaters showcasing traveling entertainers. There were also professional services offered downtown, such as architects, carpenters, painters, dentists, doctors, insurance agents, stock dealers, masons, auctioneers, gunsmiths, grain dealers, gardeners, plumbers, real estate agents, photographers, accountants,

Calling card for Bachtold & Achermann. *Courtesy of Joe Drazan, the Bygone Walla Walla Project.*

Calling card for John H. Kelly. *Courtesy of Joe Drazan, The Bygone Walla Walla Project.*

"undertakers" and, by 1882, fifteen attorneys. Walla Walla had three area newspapers that reported the latest local, regional and national news.

Around the States, from 1868 to 1913, 90 percent of all revenue came from taxes on liquor, beer, wine and tobacco, and Walla Walla was no

HARRY HOWARD,

No. 13 East Main Street, bet. First and Second.

WALLA WALLA.

——————

FINE IMPORTED AND DOMESTIC

WINES, LIQUORS AND CIGARS!

ALSO A FINE BILLIARD TABLE.

Calling Card for Harry Howard. Wines, Liquors and Cigars (Also a Fine Billiard Table). *Courtesy of Joe Drazan, the Bygone Walla Walla Project.*

The Opera..

PETER VEIT, Prop.

Wines, Liquors and Cigars

——————

THE ONLY BOWLING ALLEY
=====IN THE CITY=====

7 EAST ALDER   **WALLA WALLA, WASH.**

Calling Card for The Opera. Wines, Liquors and Cigars. "The Only Bowling Alley in the City." Peter Veit, Proprietor. *Courtesy of Joe Drazan, the Bygone Walla Walla Project.*

different. Saloon business was the most active, and the revenue from it was essential to the life of the town. In 1866, the city revenue was $15,358.97, of which $9,135.13 was from the licensing of liquor sales and gambling tables.

As an example of the local liquor and cigar stores, in an 1876 edition of the *Walla Walla Statesman* newspaper, there were two advertisements of stores selling wine: Stone and Tatro (owners, Frank Stone and L.T. Tatro), located on Main Street opposite the St. Louis Hotel, and the City Brewery (proprietor, John H. Stahl), located on Second Avenue.

By the 1890s, the wine and liquor retail and wholesale establishments had grown to about eight other wine and liquor stores, and the most noted was Bachtold & Achermann, sole agents of the Sutter Home Vineyard Wines from California (Sutter Home was founded in 1874), located at 15 Main Street, between Second and Third Avenues. Bachtold & Achermann also kept a large cellar in its basement with large barrels filled with other California wines. Other wine and liquor stores set up business in downtown on Main Street, including John H. Kelly and A. Schwarz.

Not everyone was happy to see the growth of Walla Walla, especially the downtown area. Along with growth came the "unsavory" aspects of cities, and the locals would complain there were "drunken and rowdy" miners and jezebels. Furthering these vices, including the arrival of the railroads, made it easier for distribution of alcoholic beverages to every community. In 1882, the city had twenty-six saloons and only seven churches. With the population at the time (4,000, two-thirds of whom were men), there was one saloon for every 150 residents.

Settlers arrived in Walla Walla as the Homesteading Act of 1862, which allowed single people to claim up to 160 acres and married couples to claim up to 320 acres, was enabled. Those settling in the valley exalted the mild four seasonal climates, the fertile soil and the nearby great Columbia River, which became a main source of commerce. Walla Walla became the capital of the Washington Territory. As the economy grew, so did the luxury items, including fruit, such as apples and grapes.

Two of the major contributors to Walla Walla's growing economy and farmlands were A.B. (Alvin Brown) Roberts and Philip Ritz. Both of these men understood the profitability of the nursery business and saw the potential for business from the newly settled immigrants.

Born and raised in Ohio, A.B. Roberts journeyed to the Oregon Territory and eventually settled in Walla Walla in 1859 after he purchased a land claim amounting to about 160 acres. He planted what was believed to be the first apple orchard in the area and sold some of his one-year-old trees at the price of one dollar apiece. This venture proved to be a profitable one, giving Roberts a reason to go into the plant nursery business exclusively. Roberts became prominent throughout the state as he also wrote articles for

The Bank
⁓ Exchange

FRED POST, Proprietor.

CHOICE WINES,
LIQUORS, CIGARS.

BILLIARDS

14 WEST MAIN STREET.   TELEPHONE MAIN 84

WALL WALLA, WASH.

Right: Calling card for the Bank Exchange, Fred Post proprietor. *Courtesy of Joe Drazan, the Bygone Walla Walla Project.*

Below: Calling Card for Geo. K. Reed and Harry Poland, proprietors. *Courtesy of Joe Drazan, the Bygone Walla Walla Project.*

GEO. K. REED,

Wholesale and Retail Dealer in

Wines, Liquors and Cigars,

No. 8 THIRD STREET, WALLA WALLA.

SENATE BILLIARD PARLORS,

No. 7, SECOND STREET,

GEO. K. REED & HARRY POLAND, Proprietors.

newspapers and magazines regarding life in the Northwest, the founding of Walla Walla and, especially, the growing fruit industry.

Roberts also invested in grape nursery stock. He purchased his original stock from the French Canadians living on the French Prairie at Champoeg in Oregon's mid–Willamette Valley by the Willamette River. At this time, the Willamette Valley was experiencing its own growth, especially from French Canadian settlers, since the area to Walla Walla had been closed off to settlement for almost ten years after the Whitman massacre.

Roberts was known to have had eighty different varieties of European grapes in his inventory. Much of the grape stock had been imported from Orleans, France. Orleans is a city in north-central France and located on the Loire River. The area is about sixty-two miles southwest of Paris. Today, Orleans is an appellation d'origine contrôlée (AOC) in the Loire Valley wine region, which is situated around the city. The Orleans area, similar to the Willamette Valley, is known for the red grapes Pinot Noir and Pinot Meunier and the white grape Chardonnay.

Two years after A.B. Roberts settled into the nursery business, a new Walla Walla settler also staked his claim in the plant business. Philip Ritz arrived in Walla Walla by way of California and Oregon and brought with him grape stock from his business in Oregon, the Columbia Valley Nursery. Ritz also imported grape cuttings from Europe and was enthusiastic about the possibilities for grape agriculture and industry in the valley. Not to be outdone, Ritz eventually owned ten thousand acres of land producing an inventory of more than one million trees, including a vineyard with twenty-one varieties of grapes. In 1866, the Walla Walla Agricultural Society was formed as an organization used to exchange information about the regional industry.

It is important to note that Dr. Nelson Blalock was also a vital part of the fruit industry in the valley. He started his career selling fruits and nuts to help his expenses as he went through Jefferson Medical School in Pennsylvania. In 1873, Blalock settled in Walla Walla, and by 1876, he had purchased 160 acres, two miles west of Walla Walla for $2.50 an acre. He planted apple and pear trees. In 1893, he shipped two carloads of fruit to the World's Columbia Exposition in Chicago. In 1897, he formed the Blalock Fruit Company, and by the Constitutional Convention of 1889, Dr. Blalock had become president of the Northwest Fruit Growers Association.

Roberts, as well as Ritz were visionaries and advocates for Walla Walla to become a center for a booming grape industry. However, both men understood the potential of pests and disease, especially black rot (*Guignardia bidwellii*), based on reports coming out of Ohio and Missouri. These two midwestern states were on their way to become leaders in the grape industry, ranking third and fourth, respectively, behind the lead of California and New York, until they were met with disease. Grape black rot is a disease of grape vines caused by a fungus affecting the portion above the trunk of the vine, though it attacks other parts of the vine, such as shoots, stems and tendrils. The fungus appears as brown patches on the leaves and decays the fruit. The fungus typically favors a hot, humid climate to spread, making eastern Washington not much of a desirable area for it due to the area's long arid days and cool light breezy evenings.

The year of recognition for the grape and wine culture in the valley seemed to be 1871. Grapes were offered to the locals, especially those who owned saloons. In the month of June, A.B. Roberts advertised, "I have on hand 50 tons of grapes." These tons had the potential to produce over three thousand cases (there are twelve bottles to a case) of wine. According to an editorial in the April 1, 1871 *Walla Walla Statesman*, "Grape culture is fast becoming an important feature with our husbandmen. It is now an established fact that grapes of all kinds do as well here as in any part of the habitable globe. Some are engaging in the business largely, by planting one to fifteen acres in grapes exclusively."

Jean Marie Abadie was a young wheat farmer in the valley and one of the first settlers in "Frenchtown," now known as Lowden. Abadie had traveled with the local Catholic priests, along with fifty to sixty prisoners who were natives from the local tribes, and was a witness to the priests and the tribes working on a treaty. In 1873, he duly swore on a legal petition with the House of Representatives his role as witness. Abadie was also known to be one of the area's first winemakers. In 1876, at the age of forty-six, he would produce 150 gallons of red wine and 400 gallons of white wine. The rest of his history in winemaking has not been accounted for. Like so many of the streets in Walla Walla commemorating its pioneers, a street was named after Abadie. It is only fitting that today there is a winery located on Abadie Street—Foundry Vineyards. The winery features a gallery with contemporary art and a sculpture garden.

Like the French fur trappers who settled in the Walla Walla Valley in the 1800s and brought with them their European traditions, the Italian immigrants enacted many of their familiar Old World customs when they arrived in Washington. For both of these groups of European settlers making their homes in the fertile Walla Walla Valley, planting grapes and producing wine were old family customs that were rich in their heritage and an important element in their meals, especially in place of water.

WINES OF WALLA WALLA VALLEY

Philip Ritz's speech in the October 4, 1867 *Walla Walla Statesman* emphasizes the settlers' desire to bring culture and progress to the region:

> *What we want most here now is population, not that kind who came with bowie knife and revolver slung to them, no we have had enough of that class…We want those who bring civilization with them; those who recognize the scream of the iron horse as the music of progress; those who see the little unpretentious schoolhouse by the roadside the springs by which our national greatness will be forever fed.*

Frank Orselli was an immigrant who was born in 1833 in Lucca, Italy. He would find his way to Washington Territory in 1853, the same year the territory was formed. An infantryman of Company T of the U.S. Army, Orselli arrived at Fort Walla Walla in 1857. After service, he was discharged with a service-connected disability, so it was in the Walla Walla Valley where Orselli made his home. By 1865, he owned 180 acres of land in the original town plat, north of Main Street from Second to Ninth Avenues, near the former Washington Elementary School. Following the family traditions of Italy, Orselli would plant on his farm vegetables, wine grapes and an orchard. The diligent and hardworking Orselli was not only a farmer and a member of the Walla Walla Fire Department but also the owner of the "California Bakery" located on Main Street and Second Avenue, downtown Walla Walla. It was at the bakery that he sold not only baked goods but also supplies, groceries, fresh fruits and vegetables, tobacco, liquor and, of course, wine. Orselli's was one of the first Walla Walla downtown "tasting rooms," and it was believed that much of the wine that was sold in his bakery was also wine that he produced.

On October 16, 1875, the *Walla Walla Statesman* recorded Orselli's winemaking progress: "Mr. Frank Orselli has crushed about 6,000 pounds of grapes, and already has 300 gallons of what promises to be very fine wine. The grapes crushed were of the white variety, and as a consequence the product will be what is known as light wine. Mr. Orselli has the largest winery in the valley, and in a few years expects to manufacture wine upon a large scale." Five days after the news of the large-scale production, the editors of the *Walla Walla Statesman* reported visiting the Orselli farm. There they discovered vats, barrels and other arrangements for producing wine on a large and extensive scale. One of the vats reported in use had the capacity to hold 1,600 gallons. Orselli informed the *Walla Walla Statesman* that during the season, he expected to produce 2,500 gallons of wine, mainly from the grapes grown on his farm. If this project proved successful, then

Orselli would expand the next year and purchase grapes to produce wine on a much larger scale. The editors counted thirty-four casks ready to be filled with wine, with the casks having a capacity ranging from 40 to 80 gallons. Orselli's plans were to produce wine from grapes such as Muscat, Concord and Black Prince.

The Black Prince, also known as Cinsault, became a historical grape in the Walla Walla Valley. This dark-skinned grape from the southern Rhone region of France was known as a "work horse" and was traditionally used as a minor blending partner along with Grenache, Syrah and Mouvedre grapes. Today, Cinsault is France's fourth most widely planted red grape as it is a versatile grape used not only in blending but also in hearty port-style wines and delicate rosés.

Orselli was a visionary in large wine production and especially in more affordable wines. His thinking behind the large manufacturing of wine was that with the massive production of cheaper wines, there would be less demand for poor-grade whiskey, and therefore, much of the money that was being sent overseas to bring back whiskey could remain at home. However, while there were reports of extensive wine equipment, there were no reports of the actual large wine production other than the wine that Orselli sold in his bakery.

Frank Orselli, soldier, farmer, fireman, winemaker and pioneer businessman, died in September 1894. He left behind a son, two daughters and his third wife, none of whom remained in the Walla Walla Valley after his death.

Pasquale Saturno also left an important imprint on the Walla Walla Valley, especially in agriculture. In the early 1870s, Saturno left the island of Ischia, a volcanic island in the Tyrrhenian Sea nineteen miles from the city of Naples. His journey to and in the United States took him through New York, Texas, California and Washington State. In January 1876, he arrived in Walla Walla, where he made his home, which went on to serve five generations of his family.

Saturno married Maria Zacarri in Italy, and in 1888, he brought his wife and three children to Walla Walla. Saturno originally settled in a small homestead, built in 1876. Later, a much larger home was built in 1890 for his family. The larger, century-old two-story farmhouse still remains on the peak of a slope on College Place in Walla Walla County. It is still in the Saturno-Breen family. The site was originally eighty-eight-acres, but years later, the farm was reduced to fewer than eight acres. In the 1980s, it was listed on the National Register of Historic Places.

These early wine bottle fragments were recovered during archaeological work at the Jonathan M. Wainwright Memorial VA Medical Center, near the former site of Fort Walla Walla. *Courtesy of Department of Veterans Affairs, Jonathan M. Wainwright Memorial VA Medical Center, Walla Walla, Washington.*

In the early 1880s, more families from Italy arrived. Saturno, along with another Italian settler, Joseph Tachi, who had located in the valley, sponsored and paid the fare for other Italian families to join them. Those accepting the fare were given work so they could pay back their passage once they arrived in the Walla Walla Valley. As immigrants often did, Pasquale Saturno adopted an American name, Frank Breen. The name Breen stayed in the family to Saturno's grandsons while other family members have resumed the Saturno name.

Like Orselli, Pasquale Saturno was a farmer, and the "Saturno-Breen Truck Garden" was the first commercial garden in the valley. As the first commercial grower of Walla Walla Sweet Onions, he was soon named the "Onion Man." He grew row crops of onions, radishes, spinach and other vegetables that he could distribute to produce houses, to the soldiers at the local Fort Walla Walla and to other members of the community.

The "Onion Man" not only grew onions but was also a pioneer of the wine grape. He owned a two-acre vineyard behind his farm. Tucked away behind his farm, Saturno built his own wine cellar. It was a brick root cellar, and inside the small cave-like cellar, there was a large wine vat, wine press and many barrels.

Today, the old wine equipment can be seen at the local Fort Walla Walla Museum in Walla Walla, and the original 1876 Saturno homestead was moved to the museum's Pioneer Village, where an Italian herb and vegetable garden have been re-created, along with a vineyard of Black Prince. The museum's new vineyard was researched and planted by a young man, Berle "Rusty" Figgins Jr., whose family would also play an important role in the future of Walla Walla wine.

Like Orselli, Saturno was one of the first commercial winemakers in the Walla Walla Valley. However, Saturno, in addition to growing his own Black Prince grapes on his two-acre vineyard, was sending for large quantities, between two to four tons, of Zinfandel grapes from California and bringing them back to the valley on railroad cars. Saturno not only saw the need for the local fort to have fresh produce but also met the soldiers' demand for wine. Saturno would sell his wine for cash and sometimes barter for goods for his and his own family's needs.

Pasquale "Frank Breen" Saturno died in October 1919. His great-granddaughter Karen Breen, great-grandson Douglas Saturno and their families still reside in the Walla Walla Valley. Honoring their family history, Saturno's great-grandchildren continue to maintain the family's historical two-story farmhouse and main grounds, in which Doug and Karen also grew up.

Through the years, the original Saturno vineyard wasn't always maintained and sourced, but it continued to flourish until a devastating frost killed the vines in 1955. Pasquale's great-grandson Doug remembers his father, Eugene Breen, pulling the old vines out with a tractor. Today, there are no traces of the old vineyard.

The settlers from Italy increased with abundance until the start of the First World War in 1914. Immigration resumed in the 1920s. Those Italian immigrants who settled in the valley continued to bring their own contributions from Old World traditions, such as large row gardens and winemaking. In many of their homes, the heads of the household kept the Italian family tradition of making wine for their own home consumption. Besides Orselli and Saturno, other noted Walla Walla families during this time included Locati, Venneri, Pesciallo and Leonetti. Some of the local Italian immigrants had family who

WALLA WALLA SWEET ONION CHEESECAKE

SERVES 16 SLICES

For the Crust

2 cups seasoned bread crumbs or crackers, crushed

⅓ cup melted butter

Combine crumbs and butter. Press evenly in bottom and 2 inches up the sides of a 9-inch spring-form pan (no pan spray needed).

For the Filling

2 to 3 tablespoons olive oil

2 cups chopped Walla Walla Sweet Onions, small dice (about 1 medium to large onion)

salt and pepper, to taste

3 8-ounce packages (or 1.5 pounds) cream cheese, softened

1 tablespoon kosher salt

3 tablespoons flour

3 eggs

2 to 3 tablespoons fresh seasonal herbs of choice (Italian parsley, chives, dill, sage), finely chopped

settled in California and Seattle. The local Italians continued a long tradition of making arrangements with their out-of-town friends and family members to send them tons of grapes, usually Zinfandel, by railcar from California with delivery to Seattle and, of course, Walla Walla. Later, with the assistance of the Walla Walla Gardeners' Association, founded in 1916, included in those railcars were Italian groceries, such as pasta, spices, canned Italian tomatoes and other specialty items that were often used for holidays.

The Walla Walla Gardeners' Association, a local produce-packing and shipping company, was founded as a cooperative for local farmers to pack and ship their local produce. Unfortunately, the Walla Walla Gardeners' Association, after a one-hundred-year history, closed its doors on November 19, 2012.

Heat a pan on medium to medium-high. Add olive oil and then chopped onions with salt and pepper to taste; sauté onions for about 5 minutes, until soft, translucent and lightly caramelized. Remove onions from heat and let cool.

Combine softened cream cheese, salt and flour and mix well until light and fluffy. Add the eggs one at a time and blend well after each addition. Fold in cooled onions and chopped herbs.

Pour cream cheese filling into crust-lined pan. Bake at 400 for 10 minutes. Reduce oven temp to 300. Bake an additional 55 to 65 minutes, or until filling is set. (Optional: a metal baking dish halfway filled with water placed on the bottom rack of oven will prevent cracks in the cheesecake.) Cool cheesecake for 10 minutes. To remove from pan, run a knife around side of pan to loosen. Refrigerate until ready to serve and then remove the cheesecake from spring-form pan to serving plate.

This savory cheesecake will keep in the refrigerator for two weeks. Use as a spreadable cheese appetizer or serve with a salad on the side.

Pairs well with a glass of Robison Ranch Viognier. This recipe won second place at the 2008 Walla Walla Sweet Onion Festival.

Recipe courtesy of Chef Caren McIntyre, graduate of Walla Walla Community College Culinary Arts Institute.

According to *Up to the Times* magazine, "Grape culture is going to be attempted at Gardena on quite a large scale. Paine Brothers of Walla Walla recently planted $800 worth of grape cuttings on the Hilltop farm. The cuttings were put out great care. Best authorities say that soil at Gardena is ideal for grape culture."

In Walla Walla County south of the small town of Touchet, there is Gardena North 2800 (until 2012, it was Gardena Farms Irrigation District No. 13), which is one of the three largest irrigators in the Walla Walla Valley and has held the water rights since 1892. Today, the crops in the area are mostly spring wheat, alfalfa seed and alfalfa hay. However, in the early 1900s, it was suggested to the locals to keep an eye on Gardena, as the area was ideal for growing small berries and other fruits, especially grapes. Today,

ITALIAN EASTER PIZZA

MAKES 3 TO 4 5- BY 7-INCH "PIZZAS"

For Filling

1 pound pasta, small and hollow shaped, such as ditalini or ziti

15 eggs

1 pound ricotta cheese

1 cup grated Parmesan cheese

1 cup grated Romano cheese

4 cups grated Monterey Jack cheese

1 pound ham, cubed (cubed salami or sausage may be used as an alternative)

pinch each salt, pepper and thyme

Boil pasta to al dente, rinse with cold water and set aside. In large bowl, mix the eggs, beating well. Add the pasta and stir until the eggs coat well the outside and inside of the pasta. Add the ricotta and stir well. Add the Parmesan, Romano and Monterey Jack cheeses. Stir in cubed ham. Add a pinch of salt, pepper and fresh thyme. Set aside.

For Dough

5 cups flour

½ pound butter, cubed and set in freezer for 15 minutes

5 eggs

ice water

heavy cream

Add flour to a large mixing bowl. If using a stand mixer with paddle attachment, turn on low and add butter a little at a time until well mixed. Add one egg at a time, and then slowly add a little ice water until dough forms. Wrap and let rest for one hour.

Preheat the oven to 350 degrees.

Unwrap dough and divide into 6 to 8 pieces. Roll out each ball of dough as thin as possible. Place one thinly rolled piece in a 5- by 7-inch pan, making sure to leave 1 inch hanging off the top. Pour cheese and pasta filling to just below the top of the pan (the mixture will expand). Drizzle a little heavy cream on top of the filling, and place a second sheet of dough on top. Fold up the bottom dough with the top and pinch both sheets of dough together. Repeat pie-making process for remaining pieces of dough. Pierce three small openings on the top of each pie with a small knife. Bake for 1 hour. May be sliced and served warm or cold.

This recipe is Chantelle Martuscelli-Guzman's version of her great-grandmother Josephine Ferraro Martuscelli's, grandmother Kathy Martuscelli's and cousin Dick Ferraro's recipes. Recommended wine pairing: Secco Italian Bubbles from Charles Smith Wines.

Recipe courtesy of Chantelle Martuscelli-Guzman, chef and former owner of Cugini Import Italian Foods.

the prophecy of the magazine didn't quite come through. However, fourth-generation wheat and alfalfa farmer Michael Ingham planted his first acre of Cabernet Sauvignon grapes in 2002 and founded his winery, Gardena Creek Winery, in 2006.

From 1860 to 1880, the grape culture of Walla Walla was growing while the European vineyards were being devastated by the root-eating louse *Phylloxera*. Wine grapes continued to become a thriving part of the Walla Walla economy until the winter temperatures of 1883 fell to twenty degrees below zero and many of the vineyards were lost due to the freeze. Severe frosts in the early 1900s phased out the commercial wineries. The gold deposits of Idaho decreased, and only the serious miners stayed in Idaho to mine for other minerals, such as silver, lead and zinc. At the same time of the frost, the Northern Pacific Railway bypassed Walla Walla with a new route from Spokane to Seattle, leaving limited access to the Walla Walla Valley, and new immigration to the Washington State soil would head north to those same larger and growing populated areas.

All of these changes were affecting the Walla Walla area, and during the same time, the words of Susan B. Anthony, temperance activist and suffragist, had reached the women of Walla Walla. In 1886, a local woman, Helen Isaacs, created the territory's woman's club, and eventually in 1889, the club was changed to the Equal Suffrage League. The Anti-Saloon League was lobbying, and Prohibition was just around the corner. Had Narcissa Prentiss

Whitman still been alive, this new movement of teetotalism would have made her proud.

According to A.B. Roberts in *Up to the Times* magazine:

> *The culture of grapes was our greatest success. We found that we could not only succeed with the* Vitis Tabruska [sic], *the native of the eastern country such as the Concord, the Isabella and the Catawby* [sic]. *But we found we could succeed with the* Vinivera [sic] *or European table or wine grape, and we introduced stock from the French vineyards of the Willamette and the vineyards of California and we sent to Orleans, France, and imported 80 different varieties, among them the Chassalas, Rosi* [sic], *Flanin Tokay* [sic], *the Muscat and other kinds that were the latest and finest. And we found here the identical climate for all the fine fruits we undertook to handle.*
>
> *And now we find ourselves in the position of the miner who we often meet, who develops a rich mine and from which he extracts great amounts of the golden treasure, but sinking the vein to considerable depth, he comes to a "horse," or slip, and he loses the vein and he spends his fortune on an attempt to recover the pay streak but in vain, and he is busted up and leaves. Another, more lucky miner, takes hold of his mine and with a few blasts he opens into the golden ledge again and for all the vein is continuous.*
>
> *Now here is where our "horse" came in. We had pushed our fruit business into the fine valleys near the mines which were our best and principal markets, and when fruit was produced in quantities there, we had nothing but our local market for our large product, so we were loaded down and put out of business, for at that time we had no railroads by which to ship to distant markets.*

GORDY'S AUNT MARGUERITE'S MEATBALLS

4 slices white sandwich bread

½ cup milk

2 pounds ground beef, extra lean

1 pound ground pork

1 cup breadcrumbs

1 cup freshly grated Parmigiano-Reggiano cheese

½ cup chopped fresh Italian parsley

6 large eggs, lightly beaten

¼ teaspoon freshly ground black pepper

1 teaspoon salt

2 large garlic cloves, minced or pressed

1 cup water, room temperature

olive oil

Place the bread and milk in a large bowl. Soften the bread with your hands. Continue to mush the bread and milk together until the bread has lost its shape. Add all the remaining ingredients, except the water and olive oil. Mix well with your hands.

The key to excellent meatballs is all about consistency. Add the water to the mixture a little bit at a time until you can form a ping pong ball–sized meatball that can be flattened slightly and still hold its shape. The meatballs should be moist, but not too moist to fall apart. You may use the whole cup of water or less, depending. Continue to roll the rest of the mixture into the meatball shape. Place finished meatballs on plate and keep them covered with a slightly damp cloth to keep their moisture.

Heat a nonstick pan over medium heat and add olive oil to coat the pan. Cook meatballs until slightly browned on both sides, 1 to 2 minutes per side. Don't cook meatballs all the way through, so you can freeze them or later reheat them in your favorite tomato sauce.

To freeze: place meatballs on a cookie sheet and freeze them slightly. Place meatballs in plastic freezer bags and keep frozen until ready to use.

When ready to prepare them for a meal, drop them in your favorite tomato sauce and let simmer for one to two hours until you are ready to eat.

Simple tomato sauce for meatballs, as recommended by Venneri family: fresh tomatoes, garlic, olive oil and salt and pepper to taste. Toss with pasta and serve.

This recipe is courtesy of Gordy Venneri, partner of Walla Walla Vintners. It is an old family recipe from the collection of his aunt and uncle Marguerite and David Venneri in Walla Walla. Of course, the only wine that should be paired with these meatballs is Walla Walla Vintners Bello Rosso, a Sangiovese/ Cabernet Sauvignon Super-Tuscan-style blend, or a Sangiovese, also from Walla Walla Vintners.

4
CONTEMPORARIES OF THE GRAPE

I have said that Walla Walla is an orchard as well as a garden and grove. In August the peach trees are bent to the ground under their loads of fruit, the plums hang along the boughs as thick as beads upon a string and the spreading apple trees stagger with their burden. The grape vines form labyrinths of broad leaves amid which hang the purple and golden clusters. In June the strawberry beds yield growing on this decomposed lava soil…The wonderful prolific wheat belt follows the crescent like course of the Blue Mountain Range.
Northwest Magazine, *October 1889.*

The temperance movement was feeling victorious as the "nicotine-soaked, beer-besmirched, whiskey-greased, red-eyed devils" as per national temperance crusader Carry Amelia Nation, were no longer visible in the Walla Walla community. However, there were still plenty of exceptions to acquire "legal" alcohol. Churches and synagogues could buy and serve sacramental wine. Therefore, congregations grew as more people flocked to their places of worship. Wine was being purchased more than ever by Catholic, Episcopalian and other Christian and Orthodox congregations. In fact, the number of rabbis increased around the nation.

Alcohol was used in hospitals for cleaning purposes, and suddenly more alcohol was being purchased by the boxcars to keep the hospitals "cleaner." Additionally, doctors were writing more prescriptions for the new patent medicines that contained large percentages of alcohol. Individuals and private clubs could still drink any alcohol that remained in their homes or private establishments.

Most importantly, people could legally make hard cider, beer or wine at home and for home use only. Former breweries sold malt extract for home-brewing, and California grape growers continued to sell their wine grapes. Due to the European family traditions of home winemaking, it was legal to continue making wine up to two hundred gallons per home. In 1926, an official from the American Federation of Labor informed a Senate committee that 90 percent of workingmen were making some sort of alcohol beverage in their homes—"they even make wine out of parsnips."

Due to demand, wine grapes were at a premium; therefore, parsnips, dandelion greens, elderberries and choke-cherries were mashed and fermented to wine instead. Zinfandel, a black-skinned wine grape used during the time of the California gold rush, would dry perfectly like a raisin and could later be reconstituted. Alicante Bouschet, a fleshy red grape with French and Portuguese roots, was widely popular during the years of Prohibition due to its thick skin and resistance to rot during the transportation process. The intense red color was also helpful for stretching the wine during Prohibition, as it could be diluted without detracting from the appearance. Before Prohibition, grapes were typically being sold for an average $30 per ton, but with the increase of demand after Prohibition was enacted, they were being sold for $105 per ton. By 1924, the prices of wine grapes had reached $375 per ton.

In addition to the Prohibition, frosts caused grape scarcity at times. To keep up with demand, Italian families, from Seattle to Walla Walla, would meet the rails as grapes were shipped from California vineyards to Washington State at the rate of five to ten thousand tons per year. When grapes from California weren't accessible, Concord grapes, typically used for nonalcoholic grape juice, grew well in the area and were widely planted during Prohibition.

On March 22, 1933, President Franklin Delano Roosevelt signed the Twenty-first Amendment ending Prohibition. Ten months later, Washington State governor Clarence Martin signed the Steele Act establishing the Washington State Liquor Control Board on January 23, 1934. Once again, life was good as wine and beer were legal, and Walla Walla families would continue to produce their wines.

On the east shore of the Columbia River, eight miles from the Snake River, was a small town known as Attalia. In 1909, the little dry farming community was a stop for both the Northern Pacific Railway and the Oregon Railroad and Navigation Company. During the 1920s, this little town had a newspaper, the *News Tribune*. It was an isolated hamlet, and not even a road sign was in

The vines at the Evergreen Ranch in Attalia that these Sweetwater grapes hang from are two to three years old. *From* Attalia Irrigated Lands; *courtesy of Joe Drazan, the Bygone Walla Walla Project.*

existence, despite its being a thriving community with two hotels, several stores, a bank, a post office, a creamery, a lumberyard, two churches, a grade school, pool and dance halls and many homes in little neighborhoods. It also had an irrigation project bringing water from the Walla Walla River into a gravity ditch and an electric pumping plant on the Columbia and Snake Rivers.

Settlers arrived from all over the United States to buy land in the area of Attalia with its well-watered sandy soil. Fields of alfalfa grew lush, and every home had gardens with corn, melons, berries and orchards. One of the more successful farmers was Frank Subuco.

The Subuco Farm was operated by Frank and his wife. They had originally purchased twenty-five acres of undeveloped land on the Columbia River during the Depression and planted all of the land with European wine grapes, such as Chasselas (Sweetwater), Cinsault (Black Prince), Muscat of Alexandria and even Concords. With the addition of water pumped from the river, the Subuco vineyard was known for perfect grapes in flavor, color and size and had an average yield of seven tons per acre. Not only were the grapes brought to Walla Walla for the family winemakers, but Subuco would also haul the grapes by truck to the west side of the state and sell them to a Seattle winery.

Eventually, the once fertile little town disappeared. The irrigation pumps were in disrepair, and without water, the citizens of Attalia started moving away. Buildings were moved to different areas or burned down. Hungry sheep ate the alfalfa, and the orchards died and were cut up for firewood. The winters were harsh, and the government surplus commodity trucks were leaving food every week for what people still remained. A new generation of children who had no recollection of the flourishing years of Attalia sang on the elementary school playground: "We've reached the land of sand and heat,/Where nothing grows that man

Right: "The Wonderful Fertility of Attalia Soil" brochure cover page. *From* Attalia Irrigated Lands; *courtesy of Joe Drazan, the Bygone Walla Walla Project.*

Below: *Attalia Irrigated Lands on the Columbia River, Washington. Courtesy of Joe Drazan, the Bygone Walla Walla Project.*

ATTALIA SOIL IS ADAPTED
TO PERFECT GRAPE CULTURE

FIRST PRIZE FOR ATTALIA GRAPES is the rule at the fairs this season wherever they are shown. The soil and climate along the Columbia River seem to be especially adapted to the most perfect development of both the American and foreign varieties.

The soil at Attalia contains the exact constituents essential for the finest grape culture, and being a sandy loam is easily penetrated by the vine roots. Perfect soil drainage is also found here, and this is one of the chief reasons for the successful cultivation of such a variety of farm products in Attalia. The entire area of the Attalia project slopes gently westward toward the Columbia, making the drainage perfect and the land easy to irrigate.

The climate in Southeastern Washington has been called "A Southern clime under Northern skies," so mild are the winters and free from extremes at all seasons. Fully three-fourths of the 365 days are bright and sunny, and although there are hot summer days, the humidity is exceedingly low and the nights exceptionally cool and restful. The bright sunshine results is high color on fruit, especially on the Flame Tokay grape.

The greatest producing varieties in Attalia are the Tokays, Malagas, Muscats, Ramonies, Cornichons, Sweetwaters, Thompson Seedless and Black Hamburgs. Many of the fruit farms in Attalia have several acres set to grapes, in some cases as fillers in orchards, but principally as straight vineyards. It costs about $50.00 per acre for planting (600 vines to the acre), including stock. The vines begin bearing the second year and produce very profitable crops with the third season.

The Ramonie and Malaga varieties from Attalia took first prizes at the Walla Walla Fair this fall (1911) and the Muscat and Malaga exhibits took two first prizes at the Spokane Interstate Fair. The Flame Tokays shown on this page weigh 6½ pounds, not at all uncommon in Attalia.

Above: "Attalia Soil Is Adapted to Perfect Grape Culture." The soil of Attalia had all of the elements for successful grape growing. *From* Attalia Irrigated Lands; *courtesy of Joe Drazan, the Bygone Walla Walla Project.*

Opposite: "Vineyards in Attalia Are Earliest Producers." Along with the soil, the climate of Attalia had all of the elements for successful grape growing. *From* Attalia Irrigated Lands; *courtesy of Joe Drazan, the Bygone Walla Walla Project.*

VINEYARDS IN ATTALIA
ARE EARLIEST PRODUCERS

THE ATTALIA CLIMATE, earliest in the northwest without exception, matures not only the products of the vineyard, but asparagus, strawberries and all garden truck fully ten days to two weeks ahead of neighboring districts along the Columbia. This fact, due to the warm chinook winds sweeping up the gap from the lower Columbia, gives the ranchers in this favored district the advantage in marketing their products at top prices.

The grapes are usually packed four boxes in a crate, weighing twenty pounds, and bring from seventy-five cents to $1.50 per crate.

The following letter received from an Attalia rancher shows what returns can be had from a scientifically-cared-for vineyard:

THE FRED B. GRINNELL COMPANY,   Attalia, Wash., Oct. 17, 1911.
                Spokane, Wash.

Gentlemen: Your inquiry of this date at hand. In answer will say that our experience shows that the following varieties of grapes do best here: Muscats, Malagas, Thompson Seedless, Tokays, Rose of Peru, Sweetwaters. Our vines are two and three years old and this season they produced 33,000 pounds per acre. With proper care and a little more maturity I believe that the returns would be 50,000 pounds per acre. Besides this we can raise corn, watermelons, potatoes, muskmelons and strawberries between the rows of grapes the first two years.   Yours truly,
                                        E. B. SUMMERS, Manager Evergreen Farm.

Figured at the very minimum price of two cents per pound, it can easily be seen that grapes return over $600.00 per acre, even when the vines are but two and three years old. The Evergreen Ranch, which contains 38 acres, is one of the best improved at Attalia. The above illustration is of the Evergreen vineyard, which is such a prolific bearer. In addition to the vineyard there are 13 acres planted to apples, peaches, pears, prunes, plums and mulberries, with an additional six acres planted to pears and apples this season of 1911. The inter-crop of alfalfa in the orchard produced 100 tons of hay and the owner will buy ten cows this fall and turn the alfalfa into milk and butter fat.

can eat./We do not live, we merely stay,/We are too poor to get away./ Attalia land, Attalia land,/As on thy burning sand we stand./We gaze away across the plains,/And wonder why it never rains."

The Italian community continued to grow. In the early 1900s, there were close to twenty Italian settlers who had made the Walla Walla area their home with row gardens and making wine for their personal use. By the 1940s, there were close to two hundred Italian families continuing their strong family traditions. Giovette B. Pesciallo was one of those settlers. Born in 1875 in Genoa, Italy, he eventually found his way to Umatilla County in Oregon, thirteen miles from the border of Walla Walla County in Washington. Pesciallo married Angiolina Elivia Parodi Marando, and together they raised six children, including a son, Bert Pesciallo.

Bert grew up watching his father's interest in vineyards, as well as his father's supplying many of the area's Italian families with grapes for their wine. Bert shared his memories of how many of the local settlers would gather at the Pesciallo farm in Oregon during harvest to collect their grapes for their own winemaking crush. It was an opportunity for the Italian immigrant families, particularly those from the north and those from the south, to come together to mingle and share their stories.

The elder Pesciallo also sold grapes to business people in Walla Walla and was often asked to make wine for others during the Prohibition era. However, he never did, fearing he would be caught by the federal authorities. The grapes in his vineyard consisted of the sought-after Cinsault (Black Prince) and Chasselas Rosé Royale, a sweet rosy red–colored grape used for eating, as well as winemaking, with origins from France and widely planted in Switzerland. Also in the vineyard was Malaga, a dark-skinned Spanish grape typically associated with sweet wines made from the Malaga grapes dried on grass mats under the sun. Tokay and Concords grapes were also grown in the Pesciallo vineyard.

Bert eventually inherited his parents' homestead farm and vineyard and followed in his father's footsteps, but unlike his father, who only grew the grapes, Bert went one step further.

Blue Mountain Winery, with a view of the Blue Mountain foothills of Oregon, opened its doors in 1950 and was the fourteenth bonded winery in the state and the first commercial winery in the area. The winery mostly produced Cinsault, labeled "Black Prince," or its other name, "Rose of Peru."

Unfortunately, the Pesciallo vineyard met the same demise as the Saturno-Breen vineyard: the "Black Frost" of November 1955. The majority of the vines were devastated to the roots. In past years, Pesciallo had discovered that every three years, his vineyard would be taken back by frosts but the vines would often recover and bud once again, flourishing within a year. By 1956, the vines had not recovered, causing the winery to close its doors. Pesciallo continued his heritage of agriculture, becoming a past president of the Pleasant View Irrigation District and member of the Blue Mountain

Blue Mountain Vineyards wine bottles from Milton-Freewater, the first commercial winery in the Valley after Prohibition. *Courtesy of Hans J. Matschukat.*

Horticulture Society. The old vineyard was eventually planted with apple trees. Bert P. Pesciallo died on November 14, 2006, at the age of ninety-four. At one time, he was known to be the oldest living winemaker in the Walla Walla Valley, as well as, until 1977, owner of the last commercial winery in the area.

Walla Walla would soon see the days known as the "Grapes of Wealth," brought on by a city father who got his start as a young newsboy and, eventually, purchased controlling interest of the *Walla Walla Union-Bulletin.* Born in 1872, John Grant Kelly created an empire from toll bridges, paper plants and major downtown development, but most importantly, around 1925, Kelly bought his first shares of the Church Grape Juice Company located in nearby Kennewick, Washington, and became the president in 1927. Concord Vineyards was planted outside Kennewick. Kelly urged his son-in-law, prominent Walla Walla businessman and philanthropist Donald Sherwood to join the board of directors. The Church Grape Juice Company found success in the California marketplace, especially in Los Angeles. As food-processing plants became active, Kelly and Sherwood convinced Continental Can Company to locate a plant in Walla Walla. Sherwood also assembled the real estate and railroad requirements for Walla Walla's Continental Can Company plant.

The company increased its vineyards of Concords in the Kennewick area and eventually developed over eight hundred acres, becoming the world's largest Concord grape vineyard at the time. In 1952, Sherwood became president of the Church Grape Juice Company and, the following year, negotiated an exceptionally profitable sale of the company to Welch's Grape

Engraved "Walla Walla" souvenir spoon with grape designed handle. *From Doug Saturno Collection; courtesy of Joe Drazan, the Bygone Walla Walla Project.*

Juice Company. John G. Kelly died in 1962. Sherwood retained fifty acres of commercial land in Kennewick and marketed the site as the "Vineyard Shopping Center." The location attracted Albertson's, a supermarket chain from Boise, Idaho.

The success of the Concord grapes in the area continued to grow, and by the 1970s, the Snake River Vineyard (Taggares Farms) in Walla Walla County, at Burbank, held the distinction of being the largest Concord grape vineyard. Many Walla Walla home winemakers started their first wine projects from the Concord grapes or already processed grape juice. Walla Walla's wine industry was a far cry from Doug Charles's (owner of Compass Wines in Anacortes) joking comment at the thirtieth anniversary celebration of the Walla Wall AVA: "Wines from Walla Walla? They must be produced by inmates or made from onions."

Among the Italian families to make Walla Walla their home were Francesco and Rosa Leonetti. In 1906, they arrived at Ellis Island from Calabria, Italy, the toe of the "boot." Francesco and Rosa made their journey to eastern Washington and Walla Walla County, where they homesteaded a twenty-acre farm surrounded by two creeks. They created an Old World sustainable farm with hogs, chickens, a vegetable garden and a vineyard planted with Cinsault (Black Prince) grapes, which would make about five barrels of wine each year. The Leonettis raised eight children, along with grandchildren who visited their farm and vineyards. One of their grandsons in particular was paying attention to their Old World customs, inspired by his grandfather's bubbling fermentations churning away on the dirt floor of the basement.

In 1977, that grandson opened the first commercial winery in the Walla Walla Valley, Leonetti Cellar, almost twenty years after Blue Mountain Winery closed its doors. The path to the new commercial winery was with much trial and error and perhaps a little bit of serendipity. By day, Gary Figgins was a machinist at the former Continental Can Company in Walla Walla, and by night, from the time he and his wife, Nancy Cosgrove

Eureka in Walla Walla County near the Snake River was part of a Concord grape project. This photo is from the *Walla Walla Union-Bulletin* from February 1972. *Courtesy of Joe Drazan, the Bygone Walla Walla Project.*

Figgins, were married, he would experiment with any kind of fruit he thought would ferment—cherries, choke cherries, elderberries, apricots, strawberries and even bananas. The batch of banana wine wasn't such a big hit, but years later, Figgin's good friend and celebrated winemaker in his own right Rick Small would tell a packed crowd of almost four hundred people in the local Power House Theatre celebrating the thirtieth anniversary of the Walla Walla Valley AVA that Gary's strawberry wine "rocked his world"—it captured the essence and flavors of the local mountain strawberries.

After his experiments with fruit wine, Figgins tried his skill with *Vitis vinifera* grapes, especially Cabernet Sauvignon. In the early 1970s, he was at army reserves training at Fort Ord with a Walla Walla local and fellow drill sergeant Rick Small. During their free time on Friday evenings, they would play guitars together and drink wine, especially good, yet affordable Bordeaux and Burgundies. They were also introduced to Napa Valley

Gary and Nancy Figgins purchased the current winery property and converted the tiny horse tack shed into a winery in 1975. *Courtesy of Figgins Family Wine Estate.*

Gary Figgins plants the first Leonetti Vineyard in 1974 with his uncles Bill and George. *Courtesy of Figgins Family Wine Estate.*

producer Heitz Cellars. A fairly new winery founded in 1964, Heitz would soon be known for its Cabernet Sauvignons. The 1968 vintage of Heitz Cellars Cabernet Sauvignon was influential to both Figgins and Small

In the bed of a '67 Chevy pickup, with a couple hundred cuttings of Cabernet Sauvignon and Riesling rootstock, the history of the Walla Walla wine industry was about to be made as George and Bill Leonetti, uncles of Figgins and caretakers of the old Leonetti homestead, planted the new grapes on a hillside facing the south. The inaugural vintage for Leonetti Cellar was a 1978 Cabernet Sauvignon. The word about this new wine spread like fire, especially after their first commercial vintage was named in 1981 as the top Cabernet Sauvignon in the nation by *Wine & Spirits Magazine*, an American magazine with a global perspective on wine. This was just the beginning for Leonetti Cellar. Their wines were in demand, and they set the standard of quality not just in the Walla Walla Valley but also in Washington State.

Today, the iconic Leonetti Cellar continues to be a family venture with Gary and Nancy's son, Christopher, as president and winemaking director of Figgins Family Wine Estate and their daughter, Amy Figgins, as manager and partner. The Figgins Family continues their legacy with a new label, "Figgins," featuring a red Bordeaux-style blend and a Riesling. Both wines are inspired from Christopher's memories of his family and being in the cellar with his father, Gary. Adding another wine to their legacy was the inaugural 2012 vintage Toil of Oregon, a limited production of Pinot Noir, from the Willamette Valley in Oregon, with a silhouette of Bill Leonetti taken from a photo on the day the first Leonetti Vineyard was planted in 1976.

The same sustainable winegrowing practices of the Figgins Family Wine Estate are also being applied to all-natural grass-fed beef, Lostine Cattle Company. In 2008, Christopher and Gary Figgins purchased a cattle ranch in the heart of the Wallowa Valley in Oregon—a sister valley of Walla Walla located on the other side of the Blue Mountains. The beef is served at various local fine-dining restaurants in Walla Walla.

Rick Small wanted to be an architect. On the maternal side, the Yeend family, going back five generations, were some of the earliest farming pioneers in the Walla Walla Valley. It seemed only natural that Small attend Washington State University at Pullman, obtain a bachelor of science in agriculture and come home to work on the family farm. Driving a tractor was not part of his dream, so he went back to school to study architecture. Ultimately, however, Small would become a farmer, a farmer of wine.

Above: The original tasting room of Woodward Canyon at Lowden, Washington, founded in 1981. *Courtesy of Darcey Fugman-Small, Woodward Canyon.*

Opposite: The early days of winemaking for Rick Small of Woodward Canyon. *Courtesy of Woodward Canyon.*

The senior Small gave his son Rick an opportunity to experiment with this new "farming," planting vines out on family wheat land at Woodward Canyon, near Frenchtown. Rick consulted with Walter Clore, a pioneer in Washington State's wine growing and research; read numerous books on wine; and practiced what he read. In 1981, Rick and his wife, Darcey Fugman-Small, founded Woodward Canyon Winery. His validation in the world of commercial wines came when Woodward Canyon's first vintage of Riesling received a bronze medal at the 1982 Pacific Northwest Enological Society's competition, but that was only the beginning. In 1992, Rick Small's photo made the cover of the April 15, 1992 edition of the nationally read magazine *Wine Spectator* with an article titled "Leading the Way in Washington."

In 1998, Woodward Canyon produced a second label, Nelms Road. This new label featured Merlot and Cabernet Sauvignon from not only Walla Walla grapes but also grapes grown in other areas around Washington State and produced from younger vines, as well as juice that remained after the Woodward Canyon high-end wines were made. The new label was developed to produce quality, yet affordable wines.

Three miles north of Lowden, with over 850 feet of elevation and a view of Oregon, Woodward Canyon Estate Vineyard has 41 acres surrounded by an additional 320 acres of land in conservation. Three generations of the family previously used the land. Around the canyon and lower base of the vines are gardens of vegetables and herbs and a hothouse for the seedlings. The Lazy S Arrow Gardens of Woodward Canyon are named after the former cattle and wheat family business from three generations ago. The garden has been certified organic under the U.S. National Organic Program. Like the truck gardeners of the past, Woodward Canyon sells its produce to local restaurants and, most of all, uses it in the winery's new Reserve House, which features a commercial kitchen and was built for private tastings and gatherings as well opens as a restaurant for lunch during the summer. The Smalls have left a legacy to a second generation as their two adult children, Jordan and Sager, both serve on the Woodward Canyon Board of Directors and have ownership interest in the winery.

One day Rick Small had new neighbors. The old Frenchtown schoolhouse, built in 1915 with the stately bell tower, was no longer vacant. In the 1970s, the classrooms and playground in District No. 41 found themselves empty of children's laughter. It had been a historic fixture in the Walla Walla Valley for many years. However, in 1983, Jean and Baker Ferguson breathed new life into the old building, founding what would become the third commercial winery in the valley, as well as one of the premier and most recognized wineries in Washington State: L'Ecole No. 41. The name has historical significance. *L'ecole*, French for "the school," recognizes the French Canadian men and women who settled the area, and "41" was the numerical designation of the school district. The old schoolhouse was going to be not only the Ferguson's new home but also a retirement project. Jean, at the age of fifty-nine, a former high school teacher, was going to be the winemaker, with an emphasis on Bordeaux-style wines, such as Semillon and Merlot. Baker, at the age of sixty-five, would be the marketing director, sales manager, publicist, delivery man and cellar assistant, to name a few of his titles after spending an illustrious career as an economics professor at Walla Walla's Whitman College, a private four-year liberal arts school. However, when he retired, he was the president of Baker-Boyer Bank. Ferguson's great-grandfather Dorsey Baker opened the bank with his brother-in-law, John Boyer, in November 1869. Today, Baker-Boyer Bank is an important and viable part of the Walla Walla community as well as the oldest bank in the area—older, even, than the State of Washington.

CARAMELIZED ONION & GOAT CHEESE SLIDERS

SERVES 6 TO 8

3 pounds Lostine Cattle Company* ground beef

5 egg yolks

12 sprigs fresh thyme leaves, roughly chopped

pinch red chili flakes

⅛ teaspoon medium-ground black pepper

1½ teaspoons kosher salt

5 ounces chevre (soft goat cheese)

3 pounds Walla Walla Sweet Onions, sliced

4 tablespoons olive oil

¼ teaspoon each salt and pepper

2 teaspoons sugar

Sliders

Gently mix first six ingredients by hand and form into 2-ounce patties. Cook on a flat to grill using olive oil as needed to keep burgers from sticking. Cook two minutes per side or to desired doneness. Place on bun with a dollop of mayonnaise and top with crumbled chevre and caramelized onions.

Caramelized Onions

Cook sliced onions in 4 tablespoons of olive oil in a large skillet over medium-high heat. Add salt and pepper and sauté, stirring constantly, until the onions begin to soften, about 5 minutes. Stir in sugar and continue to sauté, scraping the browned bits off the bottom of the pan frequently, until the onions are golden brown, about 20 minutes.

Recommended wine pairing: Leonetti Cellar Walla Walla Valley Sangiovese.

*Lostine Cattle Company is all-natural grass-fed beef and owned by the Figgins Family Wine Estate.

Recipe courtesy of Figgins Family Wine Estate.

Founders of L'Ecole No. 41, Jean and Baker Ferguson, in 1983. *Courtesy of L'Ecole No. 41.*

The Fergusons' first crush was in 1983, and by 1989, the Fergusons' retirement project grew as the second generation of their family, Jean and Baker's daughter and son-in-law, Megan and Marty Clubb, became the new proprietors of the winery. Megan would eventually follow in her father's footsteps and become president and CEO of Baker-Boyer Bank. Marty became the general manager and winemaker and led the small artisan winery to new heights—it would eventually produce more than forty thousand cases of wine annually, selling across the nation and in international markets. Marty also became involved in many important vineyard projects in the valley, such as becoming a managing partner in Seven Hills Vineyard and the SeVein Vineyard development located in the Walla Walla Valley, along with partners, Gary Figgins of Leonetti Cellar and Norm McKibben of Pepper Bridge Winery.

Jean Ferguson passed away in 1998, and Baker followed her in 2005. Today, their legacy is passed on to a third generation, their adult grandchildren, Rebecca and Riley Clubb, children of Megan and Marty. One can still stride up the long sidewalk to the large, heavy, carved doors with a feeling of reverence and trepidation—as if it were the first day of school—while imagining generations of children playing on the manicured grounds.

An artist's sketch of L'Ecole No. 41. *L'ecole* is French for "the school," and the winery is located in School District 41. *Courtesy of L'Ecole No. 41.*

Another neighbor of Small's and the Fergusons', down the road in the country setting of Lowden, or "Frenchtown," was Eric Rindal and his former wife, Janet Byerley. Eric grew up in the Seattle area before he met longtime resident Janet, who had strong ties to the Walla Walla farming community. It just so happened that the Byerley family were friends with the Fergusons, and Eric found himself with a job as a cellar "rat" for the Fergusons at L'Ecole No. 41. In 1983, the Rindals formed the fourth winery in the valley, known as Waterbrook. In 1983, they produced a Chardonnay, and in 1984, their first red vintages were Cabernet Sauvignon and Merlot. Through the years, their production grew, along with a popular tasting room downtown Walla

Walla at Main Street and First Avenue. In 2005, Waterbrook hired John Freeman as head winemaker. In December 2006, Rindal sold Waterbrook Winery to Precept Winery, the Northwest's largest private wine company. Precept Winery retained Freeman as its head winemaker for Waterbrook and has continued production near Frenchtown, including an individual tasting room for Waterbrook and a larger production facility for some of its other Washington brands from its diverse portfolio.

It wasn't just the west side of Walla Walla County at Lowden where there was movement of the vines. Tucked away in the northeast corner in the foothills of the Blue Mountains, about thirteen miles from the city, lies an unassuming landmark with humble beginnings. Biscuit Ridge Vineyards was planted in 1982 by Jack and Helen Durham. The 1,700-foot elevation, one of the highest vineyards in the Walla Walla AVA (American Viticulture Area) was planted in Gewürztraminer, a pink grape with Germanic roots that produces an aromatic white wine. This modest eight-acre vineyard would be one of the original vineyards in the Walla Walla Valley that was used to define the AVA boundary in 1984. Sometime in the beginning of the 1990s, the Durhams planted about two and a half acres of Pinot Noir grape, as well.

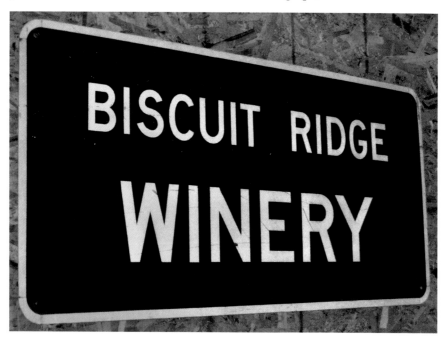

The sign of the former Biscuit Ridge Winery, founded by Jack and Helen Durham in 1982. The winery was purchased in 1998 by Duane and Mary Wollmuth. *Courtesy of Duane Wollmuth.*

Jack Durham died in 1991, and Helen remained on their farm and continued to sell their Biscuit Ridge wine that Jack had bottled. Helen died in 1998. After Helen's death, Berle "Rusty" Figgins Jr., younger brother of Gary Figgins, lived on the Durham estate for a few months. Rusty was also a winemaker, as well as a master distiller. In 1994, Rusty became the founding partner and winemaker of Glen Fiona, one of the first wineries in the valley to focus on premium Syrah.

In the early spring of 1998, Duane and Mary Wollmuth purchased Biscuit Ridge Vineyards and made it their home. Duane Wollmuth was no stranger to vines and wines. In 1999, Duane and former partners Steve Ahler and Bud Stocking established Three Rivers Winery, one of the first state-of-the-art wineries in the Walla Walla Valley. Ten years later, the trio would sell the winery to Foley Family Wines in California.

The old Gewürztraminer vineyard at Biscuit Ridge was overgrown with thick bramble bushes and hadn't been tended to since Jack died. Rusty Figgins convinced Duane that he could bring the vineyard back to life, and that is exactly what Duane did. From March to June 1998, Duane would use every bit of daylight hour, seven days a week working on the vineyard, grounds and buildings of Biscuit Ridge. He replanted and replaced many of the vines with Gewürztraminer, especially the Pinot Noir, which had been taken by deer and damaged by powdery mildew (and at the time, there wasn't much of a demand for Pinot Noir in the valley). The Gewürztraminer flourished, and Three Rivers Winery used it for ten vintages of its Late Harvest Gewürztraminer until the winery sold. Eventually, the Wollmuths removed much of the vineyard, keeping one and a half acres of Gewürztraminer. Duane gained a deep sense of appreciation for what the Durhams had built at Biscuit Ridge without the excess dollars, tools and the knowledge of vineyard care. After a long day of working at the vineyard, Duane felt as if Jack Durham was at his side thanking Duane for keeping his dream alive. Today Duane Wollmuth is the executive director of the Walla Walla Valley Wine Alliance.

In 1998, Gary Figgins's neighbor and co-worker at Continental Can Company Mike Paul also joined the ranks of young pioneer winemakers of the Walla Walla Valley. In 1988, Patrick M. Paul Vineyards was formed, producing small lots of Cabernet Sauvignon, Merlot and most known for its Cabernet Franc. Paul became an "ambassador" for the wines of the Walla Walla Valley, sharing his experiences as well as helping others with their own wine projects. He was one of the original founding members of the Walla Walla Valley Wine Alliance and co-host of a local radio talk show called

On the Grapevine. Patrick M. Paul Vineyards closed shortly after Mike Paul succumbed to cancer in January 2009. He was fifty-eight years old.

Wineries were beginning to pop up and were relying on vineyards in the Yakima and Columbia Valleys for their grapes. In 1980, the stage was set for one of the most prestigious vineyards to arrive in the valley—but the prestigious acclaim was probably the farthest thing from two local physicians' minds. In 1980, Dr. Herbert Hendrix established the Seven Hills Vineyard out of an alfalfa field on his family farm beneath a ridge on the Oregon side of the Walla Walla Valley near Milton-Freewater. The first five acres were planted with Cabernet Sauvignon, and by 1983, Dr. Hendrix took on a new partner, Dr. James McClellan. They expanded the Seven Hills "Old Block" Vineyard, and in 1988, they established Seven Hills Winery with McClellan's son, Casey, as the winemaker. Their focus was on Merlot, Cabernet Sauvignon and Syrah. The Hendricks family would eventually sell their share of the winery and part of their vineyard holdings to the McClellans and the Seven Hills name to Norman McKibben. Today, this vineyard is the heart of the SeVein Partnership (see Chapter 7).

Casey McClellan was not a soft-handed city slicker when it came to farming. He had grown up around orchards and had a sense of agriculture, so when it came time to assist his father in planting vineyards, it just made sense. Casey went on to receive his degree in pharmaceutical studies at the University of Washington, where he met his wife-to-be and "new winery partner," Vicky. After their wedding, Casey continued his education in enology and viticulture at the University of California–Davis.

In 2000, the McClellans moved their winery from the Oregon side of the valley to the historic Whitehouse-Crawford building located in downtown Walla Walla. The old brick building was built in 1904 and previously had been an old woodworking mill. Today, Casey McClellan continues to play an important role in establishing the region's reputation for world-class winemaking.

In the sale between the Hendricks and McClellan families, Scott Hendricks, son of Dr. Hendrix, formed Windrow Vineyards. It was an eighteen-acre block from the Seven Hills Old Block. In June 2007, the old vineyard was sold to Doug and Jan Roskelley and Mike Tembruell. The partnership was named Tero Estates, a combination of their names: TEmbreull and ROskelley. Tero continued with the addition of vineyards and production of wine on the historic property. The Tero partnership also added to its portfolio the wines of Flying Trout in 2008, keeping on former owner, Ashley Trout, as winemaker. Also in 2013, Tero added Waters Winery to its portfolio of wines, along with obtaining Waters' original winemaker, Jamie Brown.

The former home of Walla Walla Traction Company, a historic brick warehouse that stored trolleys and would serve as passenger service between Walla Walla and Milton-Freewater until 1931, got a new lease on life when Canoe Ridge Winery opened its doors in 1994. The story of Canoe Ridge began in 1989, when a group of farmers and other businessmen from Walla Walla, as well as other farmers in Washington State, partnered with Sandpiper Farms in Prosser, Washington. The owner of Sandpiper, Pat Tucker, planted forty-four acres of Cabernet Sauvignon and Merlot on his land at Paterson, Washington. Many of the early contributors to the founding group were also owners of significant wineries of Walla Walla, including Jim Abajian of Forgeron Cellars, Gary Bergevin of Bergevin Lane, Norm McKibben of Pepper Bridge Winery and Amavi Cellars, Rick Small of Woodward Canyon and Terry Tucker of Reininger Winery. The shareholders forged a partnership with the Chalone Wine Group in Napa, California, for a vineyard expansion and the new winery in Walla Walla. John Abbott, formerly with Chalone in California, was appointed as winemaker. In 2001, Chalone Group bought out its minority members, and in June 2010, its corporate parent Diageo, the world's leading premium drink giant with a collection of alcohol beverages that includes Guinness, Johnnie Walker and Smirnoff, closed the Walla Walla Canoe Ridge tasting room and winery. In 2011, Precept Wine Company, the Northwest's largest private wine company, purchased the winery and reopened it with Bill Murray, formerly of Chalone, as the winemaker.

In 2002, former Canoe Ridge winemaker John Abbott, known for his wine and music pairings, and former Canoe Ridge marketing manager, Molly Galt Abbott, partnered with Ken and Ginger Harrison and opened Abeja Winery and Inn. It is located on thirty-two acres in the foothills of the Blue Mountains. Abeja is located in the turn-of-the-century Kibler family farmstead, where the original outbuildings are now part of the winery and guest accommodations. The beautifully appointed winery itself is housed in a former mule and horse barn and focuses on estate Cabernet Sauvignon, Syrah and Chardonnay.

"Stormin' Norman," as he is known to his friends and colleagues, was not ready to rest and relax after retiring after twenty-five years as a civil engineer. Norm McKibben moved to Walla Walla in 1985 to become an apple farmer and assist friends who had a fruit-packing house. Instead of the orchards, it was the vineyards that captured his interest. In 1989, McKibben planted his first vineyard, with encouragement from his wife, Virginia, and their eldest son, Shane. In 1991, an addition of

Cabernet Sauvignon and Merlot were planted next to his orchard, as well as his purchase of the twenty-acre original old block of the Seven Hills Vineyard in 1994. McKibben developed a partnership with Gary Figgins, Marty Clubb and Bob Rupar, and together in 1997–98, they increased the Seven Hills Vineyard to over two hundred acres. In 1998, the prestigious Pepper Bridge Winery was founded by McKibben and partner Ray Goff.

Pepper Bridge Winery is a state-of-the-art facility using a gravity-flow system during crush and embracing sustainability practices in the

Dunham Dog Biscuits

2 ½ cups whole wheat flour

½ cup nonfat dry milk

1 teaspoon each sugar and salt

6 tablespoons flaxseed oil

1 egg

1 teaspoon garlic powder

½ cup cold water

Mix together all ingredients. Dough should form a ball. If too dry, add additional cold water 1 teaspoon at a time. Knead for 3 minutes on a floured board. Roll dough out to ½-inch thickness and cut into dog bones with sharp knife or a cookie cutter. Bake on a lightly greased cookie sheet for 30 minutes at 350 degrees. Allow to cool before serving.

Recommended pairing: a bowl of fresh water for the dog, and a glass of Three-Legged Red—a table red wine, named for Eric Dunham's beloved dog, Port—for you. In 1994, Eric rescued the badly injured puppy from the wrath of a pit bull. The pup lost a front leg but found a home with Eric, winemaker and son of winery owners Mike and Joanne Dunham. With only three legs, and two on the port side, Eric named his new best friend Port. Port was a favorite with winery visitors up until his death in May 2008 at the grand old age of fourteen.

Recipe courtesy of Joanne Dunham, owner of Dunham Cellars.

vineyards while producing high-end wines. Goff was not an amateur in this industry, as he had been with Anheuser-Busch Companies for thirty years as vice-president of corporate purchasing and president of the company's agricultural subsidiary.

McKibben's interest in vineyards continued to grow as he partnered with Walla Walla native son Michael Murr. They developed Les Collines Vineyard, a three-hundred-acre estate in Washington's southeastern corner with elevations as high as 1,380 feet. Named Les Collines, a French term meaning "the foothills," the vineyard lies at the base of the Blue Mountains.

PORK TENDERLOIN WITH HABANERO PLUM SAUCE

4 pork tenderloins (about 1 pound each)

prosciutto ham (enough to wrap each tenderloin)

2 pounds fresh plums or 2 cans plums, pitted and sliced in half

¼ cup rice wine vinegar

½ teaspoon onion salt

½ teaspoon salt

1 tablespoon fresh grated ginger root

1 habanero pepper, seeded and chopped

½ cup sugar

1 cup white wine

1 shallot, chopped

4 cloves garlic, minced

Note: Tenderloins may be cooked on the grill or baked in a 375-degree oven.

Wrap each tenderloin in prosciutto ham and set aside. Combine plums, rice wine vinegar, onion salt, salt, ginger, habanero pepper, sugar and white wine, set aside. Brown chopped shallot and garlic in olive oil. Add the plum mixture to shallots and garlic. Simmer the mixture until thick, about 15 to 20 minutes. Use half the sauce to baste and coat meat. Bake in oven or on grill until pork reaches internal temperature of 160 degrees, about 35 to 45 minutes. Cut into medallions and serve with remaining sauce.

Recommended wine pairing: Dunham Cellars Columbia Valley Syrah

Courtesy of Eric Dunham, owner and senior winemaker of Dunham Cellars

---

SLOW-BRAISED LOSTINE SHORT RIBS

1 bottle Cabernet Sauvignon wine

2 tablespoons vegetable oil

6 Lostine Cattle Company* Short Ribs (about one package)

salt, enough to coat ribs

1 teaspoon black peppercorns, crushed

2 tablespoons flour

10 garlic cloves, peeled

8 shallots, trimmed, rinsed, split and dried

2 medium organic carrots, peeled, trimmed and cut into 1-inch lengths

2 ribs organic celery, peeled, trimmed and cut into 1-inch lengths

1 medium leek, white and green parts only, coarsely chopped

6 Italian parsley sprigs

2 thyme sprigs

2 bay leaves

2 tablespoons tomato paste

2 quarts unsalted organic beef or chicken stock

1 teaspoon freshly ground white pepper

Pour the wine into a large saucepan and bring to a boil over high heat. Continue boiling until the liquid reduces to half its original volume, 20 to 30 minutes. Remove from the heat and set aside.

Center a rack in the oven and preheat the oven to 350 degrees.

Heat the oil over medium-high in a Dutch oven or large casserole dish large enough to hold 6 ribs.

Season the ribs all over with salt and the crushed pepper. Dust the ribs with flour and then, when the oil is hot, slip the ribs into the pot and sear for 4 to 5 minutes on each side, until well browned.

Transfer the browned ribs to a plate. Remove all but 1 tablespoon of fat from the pot; lower the heat to medium, and toss in the vegetables and herbs. Brown the vegetables lightly, 5 to 7 minutes, then stir in the tomato paste and cook for 1 minute to blend. Add the reduced wine, browned ribs, stock and white pepper to the pot.

Bring to a boil; cover the pot tightly, and slide it into the oven to braise for about 2½ hours, or until the ribs are tender enough to be easily pierced with a fork. Every 30 minutes or so, lift the lid and skim and discard whatever fat may have bubbled up to the surface.

For presentation, using six heated serving plates, place one rib in the center of each plate. Serve with a spring-inspired vegetable risotto.

Recommended wine pairing: Figgins Walla Walla Valley Estate Red Wine, a blend of Cabernet Sauvignon, Petite Verdot and Merlot.

*Lostine Cattle Company is all-natural grass-fed beef and owned by the Figgins Family Wine Estate.

Recipe courtesy of Figgins Family Wine Estate.

At this time the vineyard produces fourteen different varieties of grapes. The vineyard is managed by Norman's son Shane McKibben.

In 2001, "Stormin' Norman" stormed a new project named Amavi Cellars. He partnered with Ray Goff, Travis Goff (daughter of Ray), Eric McKibben (Norm's son) and Pepper Bridge Winery's winemaker, Jean-François Pellet. Born and raised in Switzerland, Pellet is a third-generation wine grower working with his father, who managed the same vineyard for thirty years. The partnership originally opened its tasting room doors in 2003. The tasting room's walls were lined with wood from the inside of a log cabin built in the 1890s that was moved from the Goff family ranch located in north-central Montana. In 2010, Amavi Cellars once again opened its doors but to a new and very contemporary tasting room in the heart of the Pepper Bridge Vineyard near the Washington/Oregon border. The sister winery of Pepper Bridge, Amavi produces affordable wines with an emphasis on being 100 percent estate grown and sustainable.

The former tasting room of Amavi, with its rustic log décor, still remains and is located across from the old trolley warehouse that contains Canoe Ridge Winery. It is now the home to Gramercy Cellars, a six-thousand-case winery founded in 2005 by master sommelier Greg Harrington; his wife, Pam; and winemaker, Brandon Moss.

As the Walla Walla wine scene was growing, businessman Mike Dunham dressed his young son Eric in his best and volunteered him to work the area's wine events. Eric Dunham served four years in the navy and later graduated from Walla Walla Community College with a degree in Irrigation Technology. It was in school that Eric discovered what he wanted to do—make wine. Dunham served a seven-month internship with Hogue Cellars at Prosser, Washington, and continued to develop his winemaking skills as an assistant winemaker in the early days of Walla Walla's wine history at L'Ecole No. 41. During his spare time, Eric was producing small lots of premium Cabernet Sauvignon under Dunham Cellars. The first release of Dunham Cellars received several accolades. Encouraged by his parents, Mike and Joanne, Dunham opened a family winery in the spring of 1999 at the Walla Walla Regional Airport in an old converted World War II airplane hangar. Eric's talent shows not only in his wines but also on the canvas. Many of his paintings are featured on the Dunham Cellars labels.

Dunham Cellars has collaborated winemaking projects with celebrities such as American ventriloquist and stand-up comedian Jeff Dunham and Washington State–born Kyle MacLachlan, a Golden Globe Award–winning and two-time Emmy Award–nominated actor. Not only would the Dunhams work with celebrities, but they would also turn their four-legged companions into celebrities. Dunham Cellars' popular red blend wine was named "Three-Legged Red" after Port, a three-legged stray collie puppy that found himself in a loving home with the Dunham family until his death in May 2008.

On May 18, 2013, after a four-year battle with cancer, Mike Dunham died, leaving behind a legacy like many other pioneers' in the Walla Walla wine industry.

It started with two close friends. Gordy Venneri was an insurance salesman and a second-generation Walla Walla native with strong Italian roots that went back to the small southern village of Serra Pedace in Calabria, Italy. After a trip to Italy to visit his relatives, Gordy shared their home Italian winemaking experience with Myles Anderson. Anderson, with a PhD in psychology, was a college professor and administrator who also enjoyed wine. In 1981, the Anderson basement became the home of a new hobby. After fifteen years of understanding their strengths in winemaking—white wines not one of them—Venneri and Anderson formed Walla Walla Vintners and opened their doors in 1995. Starting with 675 cases, their production grew to 5,000 cases with a focus on rich red wines, such as Cabernet Sauvignon, Merlot, Cabernet Franc and, of course, a few Italian-influenced wines.

Bunchgrass Winery became the eleventh bonded winery in Walla Walla producing its first vintage in 1997. The winery is appropriately named for the native landscape of eastern Washington. Founded by Roger Cockerline, a retired educator and longtime Walla Walla resident, his interest in wine began in the 1980s when he started making wines with friends Gordy Venneri and Myles Anderson (Walla Walla Vintners), as well as planted a small vineyard. The Bunchgrass production focused on small-lot wines, making around eight hundred cases annually. Cockerline decided to slow down and pass the Bunchgrass torch. He still remains as founding partner but has taken on a partnership with locals Tom Olander, Barb Commare and Gordy Venneri.

The fathers of the wine industry serendipitously set the stage, and Walla Walla was never the same.

5

WHEAT, SWEETS AND FOOTBALL PLAYERS

Drink wine. This is life eternal. This is all that youth will give you. It is the season for wine, roses and drunken friends. Be happy for this moment. This moment is your life.
—*Omar Khayyam*

The wine industry in Walla Walla grew immensely from 1998 to 2001. It gave opportunities to individuals in all stages in life: first-time employees looking for careers, the middle-aged wine connoisseurs seeking career changes and retirees wanting a quieter lifestyle and new hobbies. But most importantly, the growing wine industry provided opportunities for local farmers looking for alternative crops.

FROM FARMING TO WINEMAKING

Francis Marion Corkrum

In 1865, a wagon train from Illinois brought Francis Marion Corkrum and his wife, Mary Jane Killebrew Corkrum, along with their children, to Spring Branch at Walla Walla Valley, Washington Territory, where they would settle and homestead. Their fifth child, Uriah, was born on the homestead.

Uriah married Katherine Williams, and in 1900, their son, Frederick Corkrum, was born. Their son graduated from Walla Walla High School

Frederick and Nina Lee Corkrum married and moved to the ranch at Spring Valley in 1929. *Courtesy of Ste. Michelle Wine Estates.*

and Whitman College, where he was the college quarterback under famed football coach Raymond Vincent "Nig" Borleske. (Today the Walla Walla multipurpose outdoor athletic stadium is named after Borleske.) Frederick met Nina Lee Moore, a vaudeville performer, in Walla Walla at the Liberty Theatre in the early 1920s. They married and moved to a ranch in Spring Valley. In 1934, their daughter, Shari, was born.

In 1945, Dean Derby moved to Walla Walla and met Shari in the sixth grade. They both graduated from Walla Walla High School and attended the University of Washington (UW) in Seattle, where Dean played football. In 1954, Shari Corkrum and Dean Derby got married. In 1955, their daughter, DeeAnn, was born, and in 1956, their son, Devin, was born. Dean was football captain for UW and was drafted into the National Football League (NFL) by the Los Angeles Rams. He was traded to the Pittsburgh Steelers and later to the Minnesota Vikings.

Above: Devin Derby does punch downs at Spring Valley Vineyard in 1999. *Courtesy of Ste. Michelle Wine Estates.*

Opposite: Dean Derby, of Spring Valley Vineyard, was the football captain for the University of Washington in 1956. *Courtesy of Ste. Michelle Wine Estates.*

In 1993, the Derbys planted their first wine grapes in Spring Valley and eventually sold their grapes to Leonetti Cellar, Tamarack Cellars, Reininger Winery and Walla Walla Vintners, wineries that already had their own successes.

The Derbys' son, Devin, and his wife, Mary Tuuri Derby, were living in Chicago when they received a call from the elder Derby letting his son know it was time to diversify from wheat to wine. The ranch that Devin visited in the summertime as a child became his family's new home. Mary, Devin and their infant son, Simon, moved to Walla Walla in 1999. Devin was a photographer and appreciated the historic photographs of his family. Using the old photographs, Devin and Mary created the Spring Valley labels that are still used today. Devin oversaw the first crush of Spring Valley Vineyard in 2000, which produced Uriah, a Merlot-based blend reminiscent of the prominent Right Bank blends of Bordeaux. The 2000 vintage of Uriah, ranked No. 17 on *Wine Spectator* magazine's "Top 100" list, and the 2001 vintage of Uriah continued the strong accolades with a rank of No. 13 on *Wine Spectator*'s list.

Serge Laville, a French winemaker, met Devin earlier in Walla Walla on a visit in the late 1990s. In 2002, Laville moved from France to become the assistant winemaker at Spring Valley Vineyard. Devin and Serge became good friends and both shared a winemaking philosophy of "listening to the vineyard," meaning using minimal intervention in their winemaking.

Tragically, in 2004, Devin Corkrum Derby was killed in a car accident, leaving behind his parents, sister, wife and young son. Serge Laville stepped in for his good friend and became winemaker at Spring Valley Vineyard. After the loss of Devin, the family formed an alliance with Ste. Michelle Wine Estates to assist in keeping the winery running. Ste. Michelle Wine Estates added the winery to its portfolio, and the vineyard remained in the Derby family.

Today, a new generation of the Corkum-Derby family is part of the legacy as Katherine "Kate" Derby Raymond, daughter of DeAnn and granddaughter of Dean and Shari, joined the winery's tasting room. In 2007, 66 acres of new vineyards were planted. Now Spring Valley Vineyard consists of 111 acres of grapevines that include Merlot, Cabernet Sauvignon, Syrah, Cabernet Franc, Petit Verdot and Malbec.

Mary Tuuri Derby and son Simon remained in Walla Walla. The choice of staying in the valley or moving became clear one day when nine local wineries went in together and gifted Mary a large quantity of wine. The barrel was the answer to her future. Mary developed a partnership with

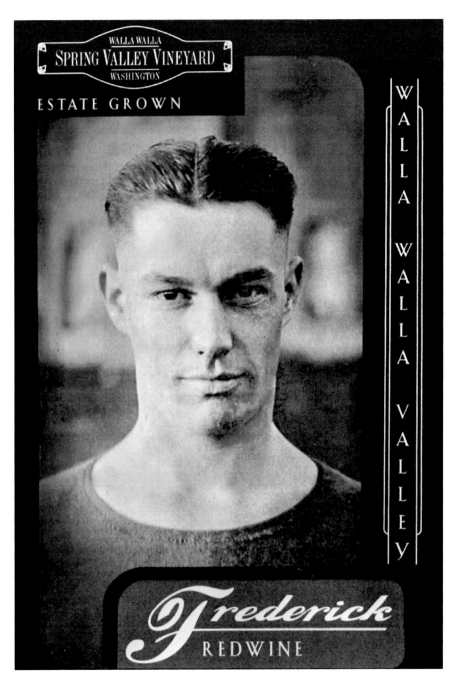

The Spring Valley Vineyard Frederick is a Cabernet Sauvignon blend named after Frederick Corkrum. *Courtesy of Ste. Michelle Wine Estates.*

Dawn Kammer called DaMa Wines, after the first two letters of their names (though *dama* also means "lady" in Spanish). Later, Kammer moved on to other projects, and Judith Shulman joined Mary to feature a variety of wines specially marketed to women.

Chuck Reininger and Tracy Tucker

Senior climbing guide Chuck Reininger met and married Tracy Tucker, a Walla Walla native whose family had been farmers in the valley for several generations. Reininger hung up his ice axe and moved to the valley. He had already received a taste of winemaking when he helped friends with crush at Waterbrook Winery, as well as from some home experimentation.

In 1997, Chuck and Tracy launched Reininger Winery, a small but functional facility located at the historic Walla Walla Regional Airport. The building was a World War II army air corps base theater where vaudeville crooners and classic films entertained the troops.

In 2003, Reininger Winery purchased seven acres of land located six miles west of Walla Walla off Highway 12 and renovated two old potato sheds into a modern winery with offices and tasting rooms. Tracy's brothers and sisters-in-law, Jay and Cyndi Tucker and Kelly and Ann Tucker, became partners. The next year, the winery announced a new label, Helix, using fruit sourced from the Columbia Valley, while keeping Reininger as a limited production focusing only on Walla Walla Valley fruit. Their new label, Helix (the genus name for the Burgundian snail), featured an image of a snail. The snail was symbolic since Kelly, Jay and Tracy's grandparents met, married and owned a farm near Helix, a rural farming community near Pendleton, Oregon, and twenty-seven miles from Walla Walla. In fact, the Tucker family had been wheat farming around Walla Walla since the late 1800s. With the Tuckers' grandfather's approval, they sold the Helix farm in order to build a new winery and create a second label, thereby honoring their grandparents and the agricultural heritage of their family.

Robison Ranch

Robison Ranch, a third-generation, family-owned wheat ranch, located in Walla Walla County, was acquired by Lester Robison at the beginning of the twentieth century. Lester's son, Jim, lived and worked on the ranch his entire life until his passing in 2012. Jim and his wife, Jane, followed the growth of the new wine industry with great interest. When the Robisons met winemaker Brad Riordan and his wife, Ruth, the four formed their winery partnership.

Opposite: Devin and Mary Tuuri Derby with their son, Simon, at Spring Valley Vineyard. *Courtesy of Mary Tuuri Derby.*

When the moment came to decide on their wine label, Robison remembered his dad, Lester, talking about attending the Calgary Stampede in Canada during the early 1900s. It was there he met western artist Charles Russell. Known as the "cowboy artist," C.M. "Charles" Russell had created more than two thousand paintings, sketches and bronze sculptures of cowboys, Native Americans and landscapes set in the western part of the United States and Canada.

Russell made an impression on the senior Robison and, later on, Robison's son, Jim. In the 1970s, Jim and Jane attained the Russell pencil sketch "The Tracker" as well as the rights to use it as their ranch logo. "The Tracker" is a sketch of the tracker on his horse following a trail. The western sketch has become synonymous with Robison Ranch quality.

Robison Ranch Cellars is located on the historic three-thousand-acre ranch. They source much of their fruit from the Dwelley Vineyard, a third-generation wheat farm that has diversified, with brothers Dwelley Jones Jr. and David Jones (manager).

Dumas Station Wines

Dumas Station Wines was started in 2003 by two Walla Walla natives, Jay DeWitt and Doug Harvey, after a few years of making wine in a garage. Winemaker Jay DeWitt refers to himself as a "recovering wheat farmer," and his partner, Doug Harvey, is a "recovering attorney." DeWitt grew up on a family farm in the Walla Walla area, and after receiving a bachelor's of science in agronomy from Washington State University, he worked as a licensed crop advisor in northern California. While in California, he enrolled in several courses in winemaking at the University of California–Davis. He and his family moved back to Walla Walla, and DeWitt assisted the Minnick family in establishing Minnick Hills Vineyards in 1999. Winery partner Doug Harvey grew up in Walla Walla, attended college in Seattle, practiced law in San Francisco and moved back to his hometown of Walla Walla to retire. The two partners fixed up an old apple-packing shed known as Dumas Station. The old structure was the former site of the oldest apple orchards in Washington, started by James Dumas in the late 1800s. Today, Jay and Debbie DeWitt, Doug Harvey and his daughter Ali Harvey are producing estate wines receiving many accolades and awards.

The Schwerins

Third-generation wheat farmer Bill Schwerin and his daughter Abigail Schwerin looked at different ways to diversify and started with two tons of grapes. Bill became hooked on the winemaking hobby after helping out at a local winery. His daughter committed to four tons of the grapes, and Sapolil Cellars was born. Today, their popular tasting room is located on Main Street in downtown Walla Walla, and they have diversified once again into the bar and popular music scene.

Lynn Chamberlain

Lynn Chamberlain, owner of a wheat and pea farm, began converting to higher-income crops, such as mint and grapes. She planted her first vineyard, Spofford Station, in 1998, named after a historic transportation hub for the local farms and one of the last stations still moving wheat from Walla Walla through the system of dams on the Columbia River and out to the Pacific Ocean to Asia.

The Zerbas

Cecil Zerba was an electrician and his future wife, Marilyn, a registered nurse when they married over twenty years ago. Cecil and Marilyn established Zerba Gardens, a local nursery producing quality plants and produce. They became founders of Winesap Vineyards and Zerba Winery, located on the Oregon side of the Walla Walla Valley AVA.

Morrison Lane Vineyard

Established in 1994, Morrison Lane Vineyard features estate wines from one of the oldest and premium vineyards in the Walla Walla Valley. The Morrison Family farm was started in 1918 by Billy Morrison, who left it to his son, Walter, in the 1930s. Walter was known for growing any row crop that could be grown in the valley. Walter's son Dean was often brainstorming with his cousin Gene Cluster, who had spent time as a winemaker in Italy. The two saw potential in the little family farm. Dean Morrison, a full-time railroader, convinced his father to set aside a four-acre plot to let him plant some vines. In 1998, Dean and wife, Verdie Morrison, produced their first vintage under the Morrison Lane label. The legacy continues today with sons Sean and Dan, both independent winemakers who have worked with other local winemakers. The four acres has grown to twenty-three acres of grapes. The Morrisons provide some of the most revered fruit to many of the finest wineries in the area.

OTHER WINEMAKERS WITH STRONG FARMING BACKGROUNDS INCLUDE GARY Bergevin, former director of Sandpiper Farms, the site of Canoe Ridge Vineyard. Bergevin eventually joined his daughter, Annette Bergevin, and partnered with Amber Lane to form Bergevin Lane Cellars.

Cheryl Nelson Hodgson grew up driving tractors and caring for livestock. She married radio businessman Tom Hodgson, and together they opened Skylite Cellars. Cheryl's father, Chuck Nelson, planted the first acres of what later became known as Skylite Vineyards.

Peter Pieri, who brought sweet onion seeds from the island of Corsica, settled in the Walla Walla Valley in the 1800s. Joseph Locati, an Italian settler, worked for Pieri. Together they planted one of the first sweet onion fields in the valley. The legacy of Locati Farms continued to Locati's son, Ambrose, and on to his grandsons, Ambrose Jr. "Bud" and Michael Locati.

Michael not only continued to be a vital part of the Walla Walla Sweet Onion industry as a grower and shipper but also followed the footsteps of his Italian heritage of winemaking. Locati Cellars is owned by Michael Locati and produces Old World styles of wine using Sangiovese from the Locati estate vineyards as well as other Italian-style varieties such as Barbera and Pinot Grigio.

It was the tale of the Wild West, back in the days when cattle ranchers prevailed over the sheepherders, but this time, the war was about the grape. It was a five-year battle with litigations over permit restrictions, but Michael Murr finally built his winery, Garrison Creek Cellars.

Murr, known as "Murr the Blur" on the Walla Walla High School football field, received a scholarship to Harvard University. As he made his fortune on Wall Street, he never forgot his hometown of Walla Walla, donating money for a sports center there and remembering many nonprofits and philanthropic projects in the town. Future plans were to eventually return to his childhood home in the Walla Walla Valley and build a winery in the same area where he drove pea combines and grain swathers in his youth.

In 2000, Murr asked that the county amend the zoning laws to allow wineries in the exclusive agriculture zone, therefore allowing him to build a winery on the vineyard that he owned with partner Norm McKibben, Les Collines. Opponents argued that it would open the exclusive ag-zone to increased traffic, litter and changes to their rural view, and one of the strongest opponents was a fifth-generation wheat farmer with whom Murr had attended high school.

The controversial proposal finally ended in March 2005, when the Walla Walla County commissioners agreed to a Superior Court ruling that allowed Murr to build the winery on the three-hundred-acre vineyard. Today, Garrison Creek Cellars, a gravity-flow winery, sits harmoniously among the rural setting as if it had been there for decades. It was fashioned after the well-known 1916 Winn Family barn located across the border in eastern Oregon.

Dean Derby of Spring Valley Vineyard wasn't the only football player turned winemaker. Another former NFL player joined the ranks of owning a winery. Best known as the starting quarterback for the New England Patriots from 1993 to 2001, Drew Bledsoe returned to the Walla Walla Valley to launch Doubleback Winery and to plant his first estate vineyard, McQueen, in the SeVein Vineyards.

Bledsoe attended Walla Walla High School and was a letterman in football and basketball. From there, he attended Washington State University. Bledsoe attended the college for three years and then decided to forgo his senior season and enter the 1993 NFL Draft.

The goal for his winery would be estate-focused wines and particularly to produce Cabernet Sauvignon from the Walla Walla Valley. Drew and his wife, Maura, collaborated with Walla Walla childhood friend Chris Figgins, winemaker for Figgins Family Wine Estate, and son of Gary Figgins of Leonetti Cellar. The first release of Doubleback was in 2007, and it was listed on the *Wine Spectator*'s 2010 "Top 100" list. Bledsoe acquired a second estate vineyard in SeVein that he named Bob Healy after his late father-in-law.

RED WINE BEEF RAGOUT

1 bottle red wine

1¼ pounds pancetta, cubed

2 tablespoons olive oil

1½ medium onions, diced

3 bay leaves

1 bunch thyme

2 celery ribs, diced

1½ carrots, peeled

10 cloves garlic, sliced

⅛ cup tomato paste

5 pounds Lostine Cattle Company* stew meat

1 32-ounce can high-quality stewed whole plum tomatoes

salt and ground pepper, to taste

freshly grated Parmigiano-Reggiano cheese, for topping

Pour wine into nonreactive saucepan and bring to boil to burn off alcohol; reserve. Cook pancetta in olive oil in a large pot over medium heat until slightly browned. Then add onions and cook for about 5 minutes. While cooking, make a sachet in cheesecloth of bay leaves and thyme. Add celery and carrots and cook until vegetables are just starting to soften. Add garlic and cook for 2 minutes. Add tomato paste, stir and continue to cook for 2 to 3 minutes. Add beef, tomatoes, wine and sachet to pot. Reduce heat and simmer for about 4 hours. Beef should begin to break down to create a sauce that is part beef, part pancetta and part vegetable. If in doubt, keep cooking and add water to keep from burning. Season to taste with salt and ground pepper.

Serve over pappardelle pasta or creamy polenta. Top with freshly grated Parmigiano-Reggiano cheese.

Recommended Pairing: Doubleback Winery Walla Walla Cabernet Sauvignon.

*Lostine Cattle Company is all-natural grass-fed beef and owned by the Figgins Family Wine Estate.

Recipe courtesy of Figgins Family Wine Estate.

Wheat, Sweets and Football Players

Westward Movement

Go West, young man, go West and grow up with the country.
— Horace Greeley

The ethereal tagline "If you build it, he will come" from the 1989 movie *Field of Dreams* is exactly what happened in the Walla Walla Valley. Vineyards were planted and wineries built, and then, young entrepreneurs arrived.

He asked his family if they trusted him. The trust would start by leaving a lifestyle rooted in technology and moving to a lifestyle rooted in the soil. Steve Brooks left his job of nineteen years at CNN in Atlanta, Georgia, and moved to Walla Walla. After Steve read an article in the *New York Times* about the new winemaking entrepreneurs of Walla Walla, in 2003 the family was packed up and headed west. Brooks assisted at various wineries to learn the craft, in addition to taking classes at the Institute for Enology and Viticulture's College Cellars. Brooks opened up his winery, appropriately named Trust Cellars. The first release was a 2005 Syrah.

In 1992, another young man pulled up his roots in Atlanta and headed west. The U.S. Navy stationed Trey Busch at Bremerton, Washington, on the USS *Camden* in 1988. After two years in Washington State, he and his wife, Jen, moved back to Georgia, and two years later, they were back in Washington. Busch worked for Nordstrom, a retailer, for eight years. Being an avid fan of tunes, Busch found himself frequenting a record shop named Ruby Records. The shop was owned by Jamie Brown, who was born and raised in Walla Walla. Brown moved back to Walla Walla in the late 1990s and got involved in the wine business. With a gift for crafting Syrahs, Brown has been a successful winemaker for Waters Winery since its opening in 2005. Trey visited Brown in Walla Walla and met Eric Dunham. The friendship between the two of them turned into a job offer at Dunham Cellars. Mike Dunham taught Busch the business side of owning a winery, and Eric taught him the winemaking side. In 2007, along with partners Jerry and Sandy Solomon, Trey Busch opened the popular Sleight of Hand Cellars, inspired by a song from his favorite band, Pearl Jam.

A native of New York with a bachelor of arts from Columbia University, Zach Brettler fled a career on Wall Street and migrated to Seattle. A lover of wine and astronomy, he became intrigued with winemaking and offered his hand to various cellars around the Seattle area. In 2001, he moved to Walla Walla to take in the area's fall crush. A year later, Brettler opened his winery, SYZYGY, releasing his first three wines. The wine labels, with colors of deep blue and orange, feature symbols of syzygy, an astronomy term for a moment of perfect alignment of three celestial bodies during a total eclipse.

They refer to themselves as "cheese-heads," these two farm-raised young men from Wisconsin. In 2003, two brothers-in-law by the names of Corey Braunel and Chad Johnson moved their families to Walla Walla, and Dusted Valley became the fifty-second winery in the Walla Walla Valley. Its four-thousand-case operations have grown to include four vineyards totaling nearly one hundred acres, with each acre expressing very different terroir (a French term loosely translated as "a sense of place"). Keeping true to their Wisconsin roots, Braunel and Johnson have implemented into their winery tightly grained oak barrels from the area of Wisconsin where they grew up.

AK's ROAST CHICKEN

SERVES 4 TO 6

2 fresh thyme sprigs

2 parsley sprigs

1 small onion, halved

5 to 6 tablespoons butter

1 5- to 6-pound roasting chicken, well rinsed and patted dry

salt

freshly ground pepper

Preheat the oven to 425 degrees.

Place thyme sprigs, parsley sprigs, onion and 2 to 3 tablespoons of butter inside the chicken cavity. Season the inside of the cavity with salt and pepper. Truss the chicken. Liberally rub butter over the entire skin of the chicken and season with salt and pepper.

Roast, breast up, for 20 minutes. Place the chicken on its side and reduce the temperature to 400 degrees, roast for 20 minutes. Turn the chicken on its other side, reduce the temperature to 375, roast for 20 minutes. Finally, place the chicken standing on its neck, reduce the temperature to 350 and roast 20 minutes or until the leg temperature measures 155 to 160 degrees. Carefully remove the chicken to a serving platter.

Recommended wine pairing: Dusted Valley Columbia Valley Grenache or Sleight of Hand Cellars "The Enchantress" Chardonnay.

Recipe courtesy of Andrae Bopp, owner of Andrae's Kitchen Gourmet Food Truck and La Porte Brune Catering

Other promising young winemakers would journey to the Walla Walla Valley. Christopher Dowsett didn't just wake up one morning and decide to produce Gewürztraminer. This aromatic white wine grape, with Germanic origins, was in his blood. His path to winemaking all started when he produced his first ten gallons of Gewürztraminer in junior high school. Dowsett's winemaking journey continued as he studied horticulture at Oregon State University; attended Roseworthy Agricultural College in Adelaide, Australia; and honed his skills in California with Robert Mondavi and other leaders of the California wine industry. He put in a few years as a winemaker for Canoe Ridge Vineyard/Winery in Walla Walla and assisted with its Columbia Valley Gewürztraminer. At the same time, he produced a barrel of fermented dry Gewürztraminer for Latitude 46, a former winery located in Touchet in Walla Walla County. In 2007, Dowsett joined the new Artifex Wine Company, a custom crush facility, as manager and winemaker. It was at this world-class custom crush facility that a new brand was conceived, Dowsett Family Wines. Dowsett's brand features, of course, a dry Gewürztraminer, as well as two Rhone-style reds. In 2009, he became winemaker for Buty Winery, assisting founder and president Nina Buty with her vision for her acclaimed Buty blends. Chris Dowsett also continues to produce his own label.

Don Redman needed a change from the life of a Los Angeles police officer. Whatever possessions, besides his family, he could stuff in the back of his truck was what he moved to Washington State, where he worked as an environmental engineer with Boise Cascade. After being in Walla Walla for a while, he took his background in chemistry and implemented it to his new hobby—making wine. Mannina Cellars became a family project as Don's wife, Nicole, and their three children assisted in the planting and pruning of their twenty-eight-acre vineyard, Cali, named after Redman's grandmother, Rose Cali. Even the winery's name, Mannina, is a tribute to his maternal grandmother, who emigrated from Sicily in 1942.

OTHER TRAILBLAZERS

Other winemakers have left a lasting impression on the history of Walla Walla's wines: Mike Sharon of L'Ecole No. 41, Tom Glase of Balboa Winery, Ashley Trout of Flying Trout Wines, Rich Funk of Saviah Cellars, Justin Wylie of Va Piano Vineyards, Josh McDaniels of Sweet

Valley Wines and Matt Reynvaan of Reynvaan Family Vineyards, to name a few.

Stephen Otis Kenyon, Deborah Dunbar and their daughter, Muriel Kenyon, returned to the area where Kenyon's grandfather had blazed a trail in history. The Kenyons' story began in the early 1900s when a young dentist, James Otis Kenyon, resided in Milton-Freewater, Oregon, near the border of the Walla Walla Valley. Kenyon's practice was struggling, and when a new dentist moved to town, for reasons unknown, Kenyon burned his competitor's office to the ground. Ostracized by his wife and presumed dead by his two sons, the family moved across the state line to Walla Walla. Kenyon's eldest son, Robert Otis, never spoke about his father, not even to his son, Stephen. Almost fifty years after the incident that began the family legend, Stephen discovered his grandfather living quietly on the Oregon coast. The elder Kenyon was reunited with family and witnessed the birth of his first great-grandchild, Muriel, who would later become the general manager of Otis Kenyon Wines. He lived to be 101 years old. As a tribute to four generations, Otis Kenyon Winery produces wines sourced from fruit exclusively from the Walla Walla Valley and in James Otis Kenyon's honor; his tall lean silhouette, wearing a derby hat, is featured on a singed-edge wine label.

Charles Smith was raised near Sacramento, California, in the foothills of the Sierra Nevada Mountains. Known for his wild curly mane and black clothes, Smith arrived on the Walla Walla wine scene in 1994 after managing rock bands and concert tours throughout Europe. On a road trip through the Northwest, he visited Walla Walla and met a young French winemaker, Christophe Baron. The two discovered they had a common interest, Syrah. Smith knew where he needed to be—in Walla Walla making wine. He founded K-Vintners and in 2001 released his first wine, 1999 K-Syrah. The Syrah met great success, as did the label. The stark black-and-white labels often featured one large symbol, such as with his first release, a large black *K*. The next step for Smith was creating the Magnificent Wine Company, which provided affordable blended wines with simple black-and-white labels. The child-like drawing of a house on the label for the House Red and House White were immediate hits on the grocery shelves. In 2007, Smith sold the Magnificent Wine Company to Precept Wine Company.

His black-and-white marketing skills have launched him into other projects, such as "Charles & Charles," for which he teamed up with winemaker Charles Bieler, whose family are known for their winemaking in the French region of Provence.

A bottle of Riesling wine. Bachtold & Achermann was a wholesale dealer and bottler of wines and brandies before Prohibition. The company's former office and cellar were at 15 West Main Street. *Courtesy of Joel Clark.*

Spring Valley Vineyard. *Courtesy of Ste. Michelle Wine Estates.*

Biscuit Ridge
Winery
Walla Walla Valley
Biscuit Ridge
Winery
Walla Walla Valley
Gewurztraminer
1988
Estate Bottled
Alcohol 10% by Volume
Contains Sulfites
Bottled By Biscuit Ridge Winery
Box 132 • Waitsburg, Washington 99361

The Center for Enology & Viticulture at Walla Walla Community College was built in 2001. *Courtesy of Walla Walla Community College.*

Above: Pictured here in the fall, SeVein/Seven Hills was of the first commercial vineyards in the Walla Walla Valley AVA. *Courtesy of Jan Roskelley.*

Opposite: A bottle of Biscuit Ridge Winery Gewürztraminer, 1988, with the original wooden box. The Gewürztraminer was grown and bottled by Jack and Helen Durham. *Courtesy of Duane Wollmuth.*

The glistening snow meets the sunset at Windrow Vineyards. *Courtesy of Jan Roskelley.*

The vineyard at the foothills of the Blue Mountains. *Courtesy of Dean Perrault.*

Garrison Creek Cellars at Les Collines Vineyard are at the base of the foothills of the Blue Mountains. *Courtesy of Jody Harrison.*

The view of Garrison Creek Cellars at Les Collines ("The Foothills" in French) Vineyard. *Courtesy of Jody Harrison.*

The former Rose Room's lobby at 208 West Main Street, downtown Walla Walla. *Courtesy of Cayuse Vineyards.*

Downtown Walla Walla tasting rooms Sapolil Cellars and Cayuse Vineyards. *Courtesy of Dean Perrault.*

In the vineyards at Beresan Winery and Balboa Winery. Beresan Winery is housed in a two-story barn, which was built in 1926 and was used to shelter horses and dairy cows at the former Thomas Homestead. It was remodeled in 2001. *Courtesy of Dean Perrault.*

The tasting room entrances of Trio Vintners, Locati Cellars and Tero Estates/Flying Trout/Waters Winery on Second Avenue at the Marcus Whitman Hotel. *Courtesy of Jody Harrison.*

Up in the "crow's nest" at Tero Estates overlooking the historic Windrow Vineyards. *Courtesy of Jan Roskelley.*

The entrance at Robison Ranch and the winery. *Courtesy of Brad and Ruth Riordan, partners at Robison Ranch Cellars.*

Outdoors at Robison Ranch Cellars. *Courtesy of Brad and Ruth Riordan, partners at Robison Ranch Cellars.*

A field of lavender with Walla Walla Vintners in the background. *Courtesy of Todd Bernave, assistant winemaker, Walla Walla Vintners.*

Waterbook Winery has a contemporary tasting room with panoramic views of the sprawling grounds, large ponds and picturesque Blue Mountains. *Courtesy of Waterbrook Winery.*

Va Piano Vineyards is a twenty-acre estate property located in the southeast corner of the Walla Walla Valley. *Courtesy of Va Piano Vineyards.*

Over the rainbow from Windrow Vineyard. *Courtesy of Jan Roskelley.*

The vineyards at Northstar Winery with the view of the Blue Mountains. *Courtesy of Richard Duval photo/copyright Ste. Michelle Wine Estate.*

Walla Walla Vintners at Mill Creek Road at the foothills of the Blue Mountains. *Courtesy of Todd Bernave, assistant winemaker, Walla Walla Vintners.*

Three Rivers Winery was established in 1999. Its state-of-the-art barrel room and cellar facilities are about fourteen thousand square feet. While you're there, browse the gift shop or play the winery's three short holes of golf. *Courtesy of Three Rivers Winery.*

The old schoolhouse at Lowden "Frenchtown." Now, it is the home to L'Ecole No. 41, founded by Jean and Baker Ferguson. Baker brought his wife, Jean, and newborn daughter, Megan, home from the hospital in the 1954 Corvette. The car still remains in the Ferguson/ Clubb family. *Courtesy of Dean Perrault.*

Cabernet Sauvignon vineyards at Pepper Bridge Winery. *Courtesy of Walla Walla Valley Wine Alliance/Richard Duval Images.*

Amavi Cellars deck with a view of the south side by the foothills of the Blue Mountains. *Courtesy of Walla Walla Valley Wine Alliance/Richard Duval Images.*

Woodward Canyon Winery's Reserve House features private sit-down tastings by appointment and a seasonal restaurant. It was built in 2012. *Courtesy of Woodward Canyon Winery.*

The front face of Pepper Bridge, a family-owned estate winery surrounded by vineyards. *Courtesy of Pepper Bridge Winery.*

The flower and herb gardens at the Reserve House at Woodward Canyon Winery. *Courtesy of Woodward Canyon Winery.*

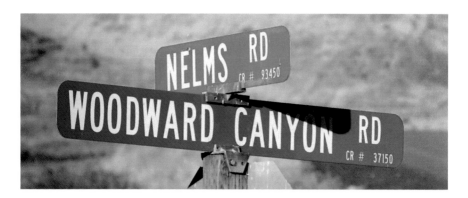

The crossroads of Woodward and Nelms Roads. Nelms Road is a second label for Woodward Canyon Winery. *Courtesy of Woodward Canyon Winery.*

The Charles Smith Wines Tasting Room on Colville Street in downtown Walla Walla is located in a converted old auto repair warehouse. *Courtesy of Charles Smith Wines.*

Ginevra Casa Smith, Charles's wife, and his sister in-law, Olivia Casa, inspired him to create a new venture, Secco Italian Bubbles, featuring imported sparkling wines from Italy that the Casa sisters grew up with in their native home of Rome.

In 2010, Smith renovated an old warehouse located in a rather quiet side street of downtown Walla Walla. The former auto repair shop is now the home to Charles Smith Wines. The structure retains the integrity of the old brick-lined walls and high ceilings. Smith now puts his rock-and-roll background to work by entertaining Walla Walla and tourists with music and burlesque venues held at the downtown tasting room.

Smith has other projects in the works, too. He purchased Substance Wines, which has a clever black-and-white label reminiscent of a chemistry periodic table featuring single varietal wines. These affordable wines were a former collaboration between local winemakers Jamie Brown of Waters Winery and Greg Harrington of Gramercy Cellars. A Chardonnay project named Sixto and a new label, "Casa Smith," a brand partnership with his wife, will soon come to life.

Today, Smith is the third-largest producer of wines in the state of Washington behind Precept Wine Company and Ste. Michelle Wine Estates. In 2008, K-Vintners was recognized by *Wine & Spirits* magazine as one of the "Best New Wineries of the Last Ten Years" and as "Winery of the Year" in its annual buying guide. In 2009, *Food & Wine* magazine awarded Charles "Winemaker of the Year."

DON CARLO VINEYARDS

If the wine lovers of Walla Walla didn't think that Chardonnay and potato chips were a good pairing before, they do now. There are no offerings of crackers to cleanse the palate at Don Carlo Vineyards, owned by Tim and Lori Kennedy. Instead, there are snack bags of potato chips for their guests.

In Washington State, and around the Northwest, a popular red-and-white striped bag is prominent on the shelves of grocery and convenience stores. Tim Kennedy is the "Tim" on every bag of "Tim's Cascade Style Potato Chips." Kennedy created this beloved Northwest snack in 1986 in Auburn, Washington. It was one of the earliest kettle-style chips and developed a cult-like following, which grew to a multimillion-dollar-a-year business. In 2005, Kennedy sold his company to Bird's Eye Foods, planning for retirement, but his wife, Lori, had different ideas. Five years after the sale, they moved to Tim's hometown of Athena, Oregon, twenty miles from Walla Walla.

They both loved the surrounding landscape of the area that was lined with vineyards and orchards. Lori came from an Italian family from the Seattle area and had fond memories of her grandfather and father's basement winemaking projects. Like many of the Italian families of Walla Walla, her family would meet the train to pick up their boxes of grapes from California. In 2006, following Lori's memories, the Kennedys purchased a twelve-acre apple and cherry orchard with a small bungalow in Milton-Freewater near many of the Walla Walla Valley's pristine vineyards of the Seven Hills area. They eventually replaced the apples with ten acres of Chardonnay, Merlot, Cabernet Sauvignon and Cabernet Franc, with more vines in the planning stages. In many ways, their area has come full circle as Don Carlo Vineyard's neighbor is the former home to Blue Mountain Vineyards, owned by the

Pesciallo family and the first commercial post-Prohibition winery in the Walla Walla Valley.

Don Carlo Vineyard, named after Lori's grandfather, had its first release in 2009. Don Carlo's photo is featured on the label. It is important for them to remain very hands-on during their new journey, keeping production small. The Kennedys are not only hands-on but also took enology courses and seminars from University of California–Davis and Washington State University. Lori completed four years of study through Washington State University's certificate program, two years each for the viticulture and enology programs. Lori is winemaker for Don Carlo Vineyard, and Tim assists Lori with cellar tasks; however, his main duties are in the vineyard and marketing their wines. They both prune the small vineyard.

Tim Kennedy's marketing skills have already paid off. Don Carlo Vineyard wines share the same white stripes as the famous red potato chip bags, with white stripes circling the red foil around the top of the bottles. It is that distinctive white stripe that viewers of the tremendously popular CBS national television sitcom *Big Bang Theory* noticed during a 2012 episode. The sales of Don Carlo Vineyard grew as wine lovers wanted to drink the same wine that the beloved television characters were drinking.

Self-Taught Winemakers

Walla Walla is steeped in agriculture from wheat, cattle and now the wine grape industry. In 1974, Cliff Kontos, a self-employed cattleman and wheat rancher for forty years, developed an interest in winemaking, along with some of his friends, including Gary Figgins.

Jim Moyer also began making homemade wine in the Walla Walla Valley and labeled it Les Monts Des Bleu Winery (Blue Mountains Winery). Both Moyer and Kontos were self-taught, and when they combined their wisdom, information and knowledge together, they formed Fort Walla Walla Cellars, named for the local and historical fort. Their philosophy is choosing the highest-quality local handpicked fruit to produce their red wines. Since their founding of Fort Walla Walla Cellars in 1998, a new generation has come along.

Inspired by their father, Cliff Kontos, Chris and Cameron Kontos began their dream of winemaking while working crush pads throughout Walla Walla, as well as driving combines among their wheat fields overlooking the

In the early years (the 1980s) of home winemaking, grapes were stomped in the old traditional way, as Gary Figgins (Leonetti Cellar) and Cliff Kontos (Fort Walla Walla Cellars) demonstrate in this photo. *Courtesy of Figgins Family Wine Estate.*

Touchet River. The elder Kontos was an influence on Cameron's life and led Cameron in the direction he wanted to go. In 2002, he joined Forgeron Cellars and, after a short time, was promoted to become assistant winemaker for Marie-Eve Gilla. During his eight years of employment there, Gilla's French style of winemaking made an impact on Cameron.

Chris Kontos also followed in his father's footsteps growing up farming wheat in the Walla Walla Valley and as a seventh-generation Walla Walla farmer, so the prospect of an alternative agriculture business had its potential. In 2008, Cameron and wife, Becca, and Chris and wife, Kelli, formed Kontos Cellars. Kontos, a Greek name, has influenced their label designs and proprietor names of their wines. Their winery is a 1,400-case production located at the Port of Walla Walla winery incubators.

Today, like so many other wheat farmers in the rich Walla Walla Valley, they are looking for alternative crops turning "wheat into wine." However, in the valley, wheat will always remain king.

BACON-WRAPPED CORNISH GAME HENS WITH RASPBERRY BALSAMIC GLAZE

⅔ cup seedless raspberry jam (may substitute fig jam)
½ cup balsamic vinegar
16 slices bacon, or more
4 Rock Cornish Game Hens
salt and pepper, to taste

Briskly simmer jam and vinegar in small saucepan, uncovered. Stir occasionally, until glaze is reduced to about a ½ cup (about 8 minutes). Cool to room temperature.

Preheat oven to 450 degrees. Place bacon in pan and heat in oven for about 5 to 7 minutes, or until some of the fat is rendered but bacon is still translucent and pliable. Transfer bacon to paper towels to drain.

Cut and discard back bones from each hen with kitchen shears and then halve each hen lengthwise. Pat dry, and season with salt and pepper. Arrange cut sides down in large roasting pan.

Wrap two to three slices of bacon around each half-hen, tucking ends under. Brush liberally with raspberry glaze, reserving the remainder. Roast in the middle of the oven, brushing with pan juices and reserved glaze 2 to 3 times every 8 to 10 minutes. Roast for 30 to 35 minutes or until juices run clear from a pierced thigh.

Serve with a seasonal vegetable-inspired risotto and Kelli's Beet Salad, but you may substitute pears for beets.

Kontos Cellars hosts a yearly pheasant hunt for its wine club during Fall Release Weekend on the family's wheat farm located on the Touchet River. After the hunt, a seven-course winemaker dinner is prepared using the birds from the hunt. Pair with Fort Walla Walla Cellars Les Collines Vineyard Merlot or Kontos Cellars Merlot.

KELLI'S BEET SALAD WITH CHEVRE AND CANDIED WALNUTS

½ cup sugar

1½ cups walnuts

coarse salt and fresh-ground pepper

1 to 2 beets (purple or golden)

1 8- to 10-ounce goat cheese log, plain

1 to 2 tablespoons butter

1 garlic clove, minced

⅓ cup plain bread crumbs

mixed spring greens

For Salad

For the candied walnuts, melt sugar in a nonstick pan over low heat, stirring constantly. When sugar is melted, pour in walnuts and stir to coat. Pour coated walnuts onto foil or parchment paper, quickly separate with two forks and sprinkle with coarse salt and fresh-ground pepper. Let cool completely.

Peel the beets with a potato peeler and boil until easily pierced with fork (can take up to 30 to 35 minutes, depending on size). Let cool completely before slicing or dicing, as desired.

Slice goat cheese into ½-inch slices. In a small pan, melt butter over low heat. Add minced garlic and stir in bread crumbs. Stir until well coated. Coat cheese with warm bread crumbs and rest in warm pan (burner turned off) while prepping the salad.

Prepare salad on separate salad plates. Top spring mixed greens with candied walnuts, sliced beets and a slice of breaded goat cheese. Use spoon to drizzle dressing (recipe follows) over salad.

For Dressing

½ cup frozen orange juice concentrate

¼ cup balsamic vinegar

½ cup extra-virgin olive oil

Whisk all ingredients until well mixed.

Recipe courtesy of Kelli and Chris Kontos of Kontos Cellars.

KARPENISI BURGER

Named after Karpenisi, a small town in central Greece.

½ pound lean ground beef

½ pound lean ground lamb

1 splash Kontos Cellars Walla Walla Syrah or Cabernet Sauvignon

2 cloves garlic, pressed

1 piece slice bread, toasted and crumbled

½ teaspoon dried savory

½ teaspoon ground allspice

½ teaspoon ground coriander

½ teaspoon salt

½ teaspoon ground green peppercorns

1 dash ground cumin

Kasseri Greek cheese

feta crumbles

4 Kaiser rolls

1 clove garlic, whole

Preheat an outdoor grill to medium-high heat and lightly oil grate.

In large bowl, combine ground beef, ground lamb, wine, pressed garlic and bread crumbs. Season the meat mixture with savory, allspice, coriander, salt, pepper and cumin. Knead until mixture is stiff. Shape into 4 very thin patties (⅛- to ¼-inch thick).

Cook patties for 5 minutes on each side, or until cooked through. Top sparingly with Kasseri cheese shavings and feta crumbles. Toast Kaiser rolls and lightly rub with the whole garlic clove.

Pair with Kontos Cellars Walla Walla Valley Syrah or Cabernet Sauvignon.

Recipe courtesy of Kontos Cellars.

CRAB CAKES WITH FUJI APPLE SALSA AND CURRY AIOLI

MAKES ABOUT 10 (2½-OUNCE) CRAB CAKES

2 tablespoons minced white onion

2 tablespoons minced celery,

1 tablespoon minced red bell pepper

1 tablespoon minced green bell pepper

20 ounces fresh Dungeness crabmeat

1 cup Best Foods Mayonnaise

1 tablespoon minced fresh parsley

1¼ teaspoons Old Bay seasoning

1½ cups fresh bread crumbs

1½ ounces cooking oil

Crab Cakes

Lightly sauté vegetables and chill before using.

Gently squeeze crabmeat to remove excess moisture. Mix crab, vegetables, mayonnaise and seasonings well. Shape crab mixture into 2½-ounce patties. Coat patties lightly with fresh bread crumbs and chill for 3 to 4 hours prior to cooking. Pan-fry in oil at medium heat until golden brown and heated thoroughly.

Fuji Apple Salsa

3 Fuji apples

¼ cup cider vinegar

1 tablespoon kosher salt

½ tablespoon black pepper

Julienne apples and combine with remaining ingredients.

Curry Aioli

½ cup Mayonnaise
1 tablespoon curry powder
2 tablespoons milk

Combine all ingredients and allow to sit for 1 hour.

Assembly

Place ½ cup of the apple salsa in the center of a plate. Lay the golden brown crab cake on top of the apple salsa and stripe the curry aioli sauce across the entire plate.

   Recommended wine pairing: College Cellars of Walla Walla 2012 Riesling or Chardonnay

Recipe courtesy of Chef Dan Thiessen, executive director/instructor of the Culinary Arts Program at Walla Walla Community College.

6

DÉJÀ VU

THE RETURN OF THE FRENCH

Il n'y a que les montagnes qui ne se rencontrent jamais. *There are none so distant that fate cannot bring together. There are only mountains that never meet.*
—French proverb

The Hudson's Bay Company (*Compagnie de la Baie d'Hudson*), commonly referred to as the "Bay" (*La Baie*), left its influence in the Walla Walla Valley as far back as the 1820s. Frenchtown, today known as Lowden, was a settlement of about a dozen families with log cabins and farms. After the Whitman massacre, the majority of the French Canadian company's employees and their wives, mostly from local native tribes, as well as other inhabitants of Frenchtown, were forced to leave the area due to the Cayuse War. Once the area was opened up again, due to treaty negotiations, many of the French and Métis (mixed blood) families returned.

Earlier, in 1838, Catholic priests Modeste Demers and François Norbert Blanchet passed through the Frenchtown area and baptized natives and company employees who were accepting of the church's ideals; there even began a competition to "claim the souls and lands" of the Native Americans in the Pacific Northwest. To inspire acceptance, the Saint Rose of Cayouse Mission was established in 1847 by Father Eugene Chirouse at the confluence of the Yakama (Yakima) and Columbia Rivers. The mission was eventually abandoned due to the Cayuse War. Once the treaties were negotiated, the area was opened up to new and returning settlers. In 1853, the Saint Rose of Cayouse Mission, along with a cemetery, was rebuilt and relocated to the confluence of Yellowhawk Creek and Walla Walla River. Unfortunately that mission location was burned to the ground during the Yakama (Yakima) War in 1855. In 1876, a log chapel replaced the mission, and the new Saint Rose of Lima Mission was settled in Frenchtown. It served the community until the 1900s.

In many ways, the mission's existence represented a struggle between the varied cultures of the area. Whether the church used fermented grape juice in its sacraments is not known (the Church of England was beginning to follow a temperance movement during this time frame of the mid-1800s). Possibly the wine used in ceremonies was *neos oinos* (new wine), which was the newly pressed grape juice or grape juice that had been partially fermented.

Today, the reminders of wine in Frenchtown, or at least a tribute to the French Canadian's viticulture contribution, remain in the old schoolhouse that was built in 1915. The old two-story schoolhouse served the area's children until 1974 and was later purchased by Baker and Jean Ferguson in 1977. L'Ecole No. 41 opened its doors as a winery in 1983.

BERGEVIN FAMILY

The Bergevin family, with deep roots of French Canadian ancestry, was among the early settlers in Frenchtown, arriving in the valley in 1859. In 2002, Gary Bergevin and his daughter, Annette Bergevin, partnered with Amber Lane in forming Bergevin Lane Vineyards, with a winery located in Walla Walla. In 2011, they founded Bergevin Lane's Estate vineyard, Bergevin Springs, planted on twenty-five acres of Bergevin homestead land from 1903 in Frenchtown. The new estate vineyard is planted with wine grapes of strong French history, predominantly Cabernet Sauvignon, as well as Malbec, Merlot, Cabernet Franc, Petite Verdot and Viognier.

MARIE-EVE GILLA AND GILLES NICAULT

In 1991, a young woman from France ventured to the New World with goals to further her career in winemaking, as well as to have a better understanding of the English language. Her first stop was the Pacific Northwest.

Marie-Eve Gilla was born in Paris, France, and was raised near the romantic city known for its food and wine culture. She found herself enjoying the country, vacationing near the Burgundy region, a historical area of east-central France. Burgundy is also one of France's main wine-producing areas, known for both its red and white wines, mostly from Pinot Noir and Chardonnay grapes. Gilla was drawn to the vineyards in the country, as well as the art of winemaking.

In the winemaking world of France, there were few opportunities for young winemakers unless they were born into a family owning wine-producing châteaus and even fewer opportunities for a young French woman. However, this didn't stop Marie-Eve Gilla from earning her Diplome National d'Oenologie (master's) at the University of Bourgogne–Dijon while gaining experience working in Burgundy's wineries and vineyards. It was a goal she had to strive for, as at the time the university would not accept more than five females out of every thirty-two students.

Washington State was the next stop for her journey in 1992 as she continued building a reputation, and she finally landed in Walla Walla and made the valley her home. In 2001, she became the founding winemaker and managing partner of Forgeron Cellars. *Forgeron* means "blacksmith" in French. During the remodeling and construction of the new winery located in downtown Walla Walla, hundreds of horseshoes were unearthed. Apparently, the winery stood where there once had been a blacksmith shop. A reminder of Walla Walla's western days of the past, the old horseshoes still remain and are buried in the foundation of the winery for good luck. In 2004, Gilla became a U.S. citizen.

At one of the wineries in the Columbia Valley in eastern Washington State, Gilla met another young winemaker from France.

In 1992, a young French winemaker left his homeland to come to America for the opportunity to be part of the growing wine community in the Pacific Northwest. Gilles Nicault grew up in southern France and graduated from the University of Avignon near Provence and the famous wine villages of Tavel and Châteauneuf-du-Pape. Nicault graduated with a degree in viticulture and enology and refined his craft in the legendary vineyards and wineries of Côtes du Rhône, Provence and Champagne. In 1994, already a celebrated winemaker of his homeland, Gilles traveled to Washington State to expand his winemaking skills in the Columbia Valley. Ironically, it was in America that he met another French winemaker—petite, dark-eyed Marie-Eve Gilla—who would become his wife.

In 1996, Nicault made his home in Walla Walla, taking his first job in the valley at the world-class winery of Woodward Canyon, located near

Frenchtown. Nicault brought his winemaking talents, as well as his talent for producing rosés like the bone-dry Provençal rosés. Woodward Canyon was one of the first wineries in the valley to introduce this dry, yet pretty pink wine of Cabernet Franc. In 1999, Gilles Nicault became the head of enology and production for Woodward Canyon.

His talents were once again recognized when he was named director of winemaking and viticulture for Long Shadows Vintners. Since the winery's inception in 2003, Nicault has overseen daily operations at the state-of-the-art facility located in Walla Walla County, a few miles northeast of the original Frenchtown. Nicault works with a group of internationally acclaimed vintners from around the world. One of Nicault's assignments is to ensure each associate winemaker's vision is realized, not only in the cellar, but in the vineyard, as well.

An honor was bestowed when the Long Shadows 2009 Chester-Kidder, a red Bordeaux-style blend crafted by Gilles Nicault, was the fourth Long Shadows wine to find its way on the White House menu. In February 2014, it was appropriate that the young French-born winemaker's New World wine Chester-Kidder would be served at a White House state dinner honoring French president François Hollande.

Today, Marie-Eve Gilla and Gilles Nicault are the caretakers not only of a new generation of French-influenced New World wines but also of another generation of French winemakers: their son and daughter.

Serge Laville

In France's northern area of Côtes du Rhône, home to eight distinctive wine regions, a young boy was sipping some of France's most famous wines before he was ten years old. Serge Laville grew up with a grandfather, "grand-père," who was a wine aficionado with a wine cellar worthy of admiration. It was perhaps a sign that he would one day come to America, with only a camera and backpack, and meet up with an up-and-coming young winemaker in the Walla Walla Valley.

Laville was a young Renaissance man in France working as a professional photographer. Laville's early training of his wine palate, encouraged by his grand-père, would assist him as he continued his education in chemistry and biology, thus leading him full circle to enology. Through Laville's studies in enology, he worked with Marie Laure Sylvestre, an acclaimed wine consultant, and journeyed to many of the wine regions in France to examine the terroir that was unique to those regions. Of course, he also learned through tasting the various wines the regions were known for.

After a decade of seeking wine knowledge in his own homeland, Laville started the new century by heading to the United States to become a wine tourist in the New World. The road eventually brought Laville to the Walla Walla Valley. It was in Walla Walla that Laville had the good fortune to meet another young Renaissance man, photographer and winemaker, Devin Corkrum Derby. Derby was the founding winemaker of Spring Valley Vineyard, and the two men became friends. Laville became infatuated with the Walla Walla Valley, from the beautiful historical homes to the spectacular colors of the surrounding Blue Mountains and rolling hills of the wheat-filled countryside. However, Devin Derby wasn't the only person Serge Laville met in Walla Walla. He also became acquainted with Walla Walla native Madeleine Call.

Laville made several journeys from Walla Walla back to his native home of France. In 2002, Derby asked Laville to become his assistant at Spring Valley Vineyards. Laville was at a crossroads in his life; he had a few life-altering choices before him. Laville said yes to Derby's offer as he respected the wines of Spring Valley and his friendship with Derby. This was also a rare opportunity for a young French winemaker. The other life-changing decision was asking Madeleine to become his wife.

In 2002, Laville started crush at Spring Valley and quickly understood the unique attributes of the soil of the vineyard, as well as the winemaking style of Spring Valley. He made use of the French philosophy, and one that Derby also shared, of "listening to the vineyard." This philosophy meant understanding that one of the most important jobs of a winemaker is to allow nature to take its course by using minimal, yet careful intervention in the beginning of the harvest, the actual winemaking and the final pour in the glass.

Unfortunately, in 2004, Devin Corkrum Derby died. Laville was left not only to become the caretaker of the wines but also to deal with grieving the loss of his close friend. In 2005, Serge Laville became the winemaker of Spring Valley Vineyards and continues the legacy of his friend. He has also implemented a light "French touch" to the New World wines, which are dominated by the flavors and character of the soil that for generations was planted with wheat. Regarding the other life-changing decision, it just so happened that Madeleine said yes to Serge's proposal. Today, they have two young daughters and reside in Walla Walla.

Déjà Vu

The Ground Speaks

I wonder if the ground has anything to say? I wonder if the ground is listening to what is said? I hear what the ground says. It says it is the Great Spirit that placed me here. The Great Spirit tells me to take care of the Indians, to feed them aright. The Great Spirit appointed the roots to feed the Indians on. The water says the same thing. The Great Spirit directs me, "Feed the Indians well." The grass says the same thing, "Feed the horses and cattle."

The ground says, "The Great Spirit has placed me here to produce all that grows on me, tree and fruit." The same way the ground says, "It was from me man was made." The Great Spirit in placing men on earth, desired them to take good care of the ground and to do each other no harm.
—Cayuse chief Tauitau (Tawatoe), 1855 Treaty Council

The ground of the Walla Walla Valley spoke to a young man who ventured to the southeastern area of Washington State from across the sea. This young Frenchman eventually gave the locals something to chatter about with his bright tasting room painted a vivid sunflower yellow, which stood out among the conservative Victorian buildings of downtown Walla Walla. The bright color was reminiscent of the historic merchant buildings in Provence, France. Later, he would give the locals more to chatter about.

Christophe Baron's roots began near the village of Charly-sur-Marne in Champagne, a region located northeast of France, between Paris and Belgium. It was there that the young boy would walk the family vineyard with his father and grandfather. Baron's ancestors had worked the land since 1677, leaving him the youngest of the generation from the centuries-old Champagne house Baron Albert. It was in his blood to become a *vigneron*, a fifteenth-century-old French title not widely used in the United States.

Baron accentuated his title of vigneron by studying viticulture in Champagne and in Burgundy, another of France's main wine-producing areas. After his studies, instead of following in his family's footsteps, he gave into his impulse to travel. Through his studies, Baron was introduced to the Pinot Noirs of Burgundy and became infatuated. Baron began his journey by accepting an internship at a winery in the Willamette Valley of Oregon, an American wine region known for its Pinot Noir. His work in the Willamette Valley eventually led Baron up north to the neighboring wine valley of Walla Walla in 1993, over one hundred years after another French settler followed the trail to Lowden, formerly known as Frenchtown.

In Lowden, Baron interned at Waterbrook Winery. It wasn't long after that when the impulse to travel took over again, and Baron headed to Australia,

RISOTTO WITH PAN-SEARED SCALLOPS AND BUTTERNUT SQUASH

SERVES 4

For Risotto

1¼ cups diced, peeled, seeded butternut squash

2 cups chicken stock

2 cups water

1 tablespoon olive oil

1 small onion, finely chopped

¾ cup Arborio rice

⅓ cup grated Parmigiano-Reggiano cheese

1 tablespoon unsalted butter

salt and pepper, to taste

For Scallops

20 large sea scallops, tough muscle removed from side

salt, to taste

2 to 3 tablespoons olive oil

3 tablespoons unsalted butter

2 tablespoons thinly sliced fresh sage

Cook diced butternut squash in medium saucepan two-thirds full of simmering water until tender. Drain in a colander.

Bring stock and 2 cups water to a simmer in a saucepan and keep at a bare simmer. Heat oil in a 2½-quart heavy saucepan over moderate heat. Add onion, stirring occasionally, until softened. Add rice and cook, stirring 1 minute. Add 1 cup simmering stock and cook at a strong simmer, stirring constantly until stock is absorbed. Continue simmering, adding stock ½ cup at a time, stirring constantly, letting each addition be absorbed before adding the next until rice is tender and creamy looking but still al dente. This will take about 18 minutes. There may be broth left over.

Remove from heat and stir in the diced butternut squash, cheese and butter, stirring until butter is melted. Season with salt and pepper to taste. Cover to keep warm.

Pat scallops dry and season with salt. Heat oil in a 12-inch nonstick skillet over moderate-high heat until hot but not smoking. Sauté scallops, turning once, until golden brown, 4 to 6 minutes. Transfer to a bowl with a slotted spoon and discard any oil remaining in the skillet. Do not clean skillet.

Cook butter in same skillet over moderate heat until it foams and turns light brown. Add sage and cook, stirring 1 minute. Remove from heat, season with salt.

Fill four shallow soup bowls with risotto, top with scallops and drizzle with sage butter.

Recommended wine pairing: Forgeron Cellars Chardonnay.

Recipe courtesy of Forgeron Cellars.

New Zealand and Romania to gain more winemaking experience. His intention was to journey back to the Willamette Valley of Oregon, where he wanted to purchase land and plant his own vineyard. However, those plans changed when he paid a visit to Walla Walla in April 1996.

The visit to the valley was purely a social one. As Baron was roaming around the local countryside near the Oregon/Washington border, he noticed an old orchard fifteen miles south of Walla Walla. The old Walla Walla River bed was strewn and scattered about with acres of stones the size of apples. These ten-acres had been neglected and overlooked through the years. While other farmers saw land that could not be used in traditional farming methods, Christophe Baron saw potential that only a winemaker from France could distinguish. The ground spoke to him.

The ancient land, littered with cobblestones, is similar to the terroir of Châteauneuf-du-Pape, as well as areas of Bordeaux in France. The village of Châteauneuf-du-Pape (which translates to the "Pope's new castle," and is an area entwined with papal history) is located in southeastern France and is one of the most renowned wine appellations of the southern part of the Rhône area. The appellation stretches along the eastern bank of the Rhône River. The area to the north and northeast is famous for the round rocks and pebbles that cover the soil. The rocks are famous for providing proper drainage, yet restricting nutrients, forcing the vines to struggle to break through the surface of the earth. This limits the vines' yield yet concentrates and enhances the flavor of the grape. The rocky soil of Châteauneuf-du-Pape and Cayuse Vineyards—which is what Baron named the land he bought in the valley—retains heat from the sun during the day, and the rocks release the heat during the night, therefore ripening the grapes faster.

The profile of the rocky soil is the "welter and waste" where the Missoula Floods ravaged Eastern Washington over twelve to fifteen thousand years ago. As the flood waters receded, leaving behind layers of sand and silt, the Walla Walla River would force its way back, replacing the area with rocks of all sizes from pebbles and smooth cobbles to rounded worn boulders that were produced from the basalt of the surrounding Blue Mountains.

Was it fate that a third-generation vineyard in Châteauneuf-du-Pape was fittingly named Domaine Les Cailloux (pronounced "ki-yoo") for the cailloux roulés (large stones) while across the sea in the Walla Walla area original inhabitants of the valley were known as the Cayuse—the people of the stones? In 1997, Baron purchased the old orchard property and planted his first vineyard. It was only fitting that he would call his new venture Cayuse Vineyards.

According to Baron, "mistreating the earth kills the terroir, and you end up with soils that are sick or dead. It's a foundation you have to protect." Baron would be coined the "Crazy Frenchman" as the ancient rocky ground challenged him, but he knew that more important than his own struggle was that of the vines. Baron also brought to the valley a new type of farming: Old World style of biodynamic farming that is used on many successful and flourishing vineyards in France and Germany.

In 2002, Cayuse Vineyards was the first vineyard in the valley to put into practice this chemical-free organic philosophy of farming that was developed back in the 1920s, focusing on the ecosystem and coordinating the natural cycles of earth, plants and animals. The tenets of biodynamic farming involve using an astronomical calendar during the planting and harvesting and other elements like composts, manure, earth "teas" and minerals, such as quartz. Cayuse crushed its first biodynamic-certified fruit in the 2005 vintage.

Currently, Baron farms eight vineyards that are spread over sixty acres in the Walla Walla Valley. All of the vines are planted in the rocky soil. It is this hard and solid matter in the soil that highly stresses the vines and brings in the desired yield of only two tons per acre. Syrah is the dominant fruit, with the addition of Cabernet Franc, Cabernet Sauvignon, Grenache, Merlot, Tempranillo and Viognier.

To complete the farming circle, Baron has added chickens, pigs, sheep and cows, as well as an orchard of apple and cherry trees and a summer garden. Eventually he added the "horse power" of two draft horses.

Meringue Shells with Sliced Strawberries and Chocolate Sauce

Serves 12

5 large egg whites
pinch coarse salt
1¼ cups sugar, plus 3 tablespoons
12 ounces semisweet chocolate, chopped
3 pounds strawberries
6 tablespoons water
whipped cream
12 mint leaves

Position one rack in bottom third and one rack in top third of oven and preheat to 250 degrees. Line two large baking sheets with parchment paper. Using a 3¼-inch round as a guide, draw six circles on each paper.

Using an electric mixer beat egg whites and salt in large bowl until soft peaks form. Gradually add 1¼ cups sugar, beating until whites are stiff and glossy. Dab corners of parchment with meringue. Turn parchment over (drawn circles will show through), pressing on the corners to anchor parchment to baking sheets. Drop generous ⅓-cup portions of meringue onto each circle. Spread meringue with back of spoon to fill circle, depressing centers to form shells.

Bake meringues until crisp and almost dry, about 1 hour and 15 minutes. Turn off oven, leave door closed. Let meringues dry in oven 1 hour longer. Lift meringues from parchment. (Can be made one week ahead, wrapped and stored in an airtight container.)

Melt chocolate in a double boiler over simmering water, stirring until smooth. Remove pan from over water. Holding stem end, dip 12 strawberries almost to cover. Place berries on foil-lined plate and refrigerate until chocolate is set. Whisk 6 tablespoons water into remaining chocolate to use as sauce.

Hull and slice remaining strawberries. Place in large bowl. Mix in remaining 3 tablespoons sugar. Place meringues on plates. Top with sliced berries. Drizzle with chocolate sauce. Add a dollop of whipped cream and top with dipped strawberry. Garnish with a fresh mint leaf.

Recommended wine pairing: Forgeron Cellars Late Harvest wine.

Recipe courtesy of Forgeron Cellars

Left: No Girls Wine is named after the notorious Rose Rooms as a tribute to Walla Walla's past. *Courtesy of Cayuse Vineyard.*

Below: The lobby sign of No Girls is on the former Rose Rooms at 208 West Main Street, Walla Walla. *Courtesy of Cayuse Vineyard.*

Baron was busy in 2002, as he also acquired property downtown Walla Walla located at what was known as "lower" West Main Street. The 200 block of "lower" Main had a history of saloons, gambling and billiard parlors and brothels. It was this downtown building, whose upper level held the secrets of the "Rose Rooms," that inspired Baron, along with his assistant winemaker, Elizabeth Bourcier, and general manager, Trevor Dorland, to produce a new label called No Girls.

The first release of No Girls wines was in 2009, a three-hundred-case production with a focus on Syrah and Grenache from the Cayuse La Paciencia Vineyard. *Paciencia* is Spanish for "patience," a very appropriate name since the project was several years in the making—the vineyard was planted from 2003 through 2005. The limited wines have received many high scores and accolades, along with a long waiting list.

The name No Girls for the wine label was inspired by the garish red graffiti left behind on the turquoise-colored walls of the second-floor of the building known as the "Rose Rooms." Prostitution was a legal and thriving business when Walla Walla was first founded in the 1860s and 1870s due to the gold miners from Idaho who spent their money on provisions and "good times" in the "city so nice, they named it twice." In fact, to operate a bordello in Walla Walla, a quarterly license fee of $500 was charged. In 1913, the legislature passed a "red light abatement" act making being a customer or employee of a bordello a misdemeanor—if you were caught. However, entrepreneurs of these disorderly houses continued to operate rather quietly. In 1951, the building was classified as a "lodging house" for mostly retired male occupants, with a reminder that "No Girls" were allowed beyond the upstairs hallway scrawled on the wall. Much to the dismay of many fine folk in the community, in 1952, *Look Magazine*, a bi-weekly, general-interest magazine with more of an emphasis on photographs than written articles, wrote that Walla Walla was among the "seediest cities of America" due to its tolerance of prostitution.

The address that was written on a door in an alley with the name "Rose Rooms" still remains. Other reminders of the past are iron bed frames, mattresses, wall windows from each one of the rooms facing into the hallway and, most importantly, a primitive hand-drawn picture of a woman with a 1920s flapper hairstyle on the wall that was later used as an image on the No Girls wine box.

Once again, with the addition of farm animals closing the biodynamic circle, Baron showed respect to the "old ways" as his grandfather did before him in their family vineyards in the Champagne region of France. In May

RYAN'S PAELLA

Every culture has their wonder dish, and paella is Spain's. *Paella* actually means "pan" in Spanish. The Spaniards are very passionate about their paella. Men have been known to have epic sword fights, much like the legendary battle between Inigo Montoya and the Dread Pirate Roberts, over whose grandmother made the best paella. There is no single way to make paella. It is all about what is in season and what you find in your pantry. That being said, here is my way of making paella. If you follow a few of my more ardent rules, you will conquer this recipe. Now, don't screw this up.

Note on pans: they come in a variety of sizes and can be purchased online. Propane burners and wood fire stands are also available for purchase. If you prefer to shop in person, there is Spanish Table in downtown Seattle, conveniently located next to Pikes Place Market, where you can find most of the ingredients for your paella.

½ to 1 red bell pepper or more (depending on number of people)

1 cup chicken stock, per person (Make sure it is good stock. If you use chicken bouillon cubes, I will personally show up at your house and beat you with a large sack of Bomba rice in front of your family. Your children will weep and say, "Why did that strange yet compellingly handsome man hurt you?" Embarrassed, you will sob and say, "My darlings, it's my fault. I was using bouillon cubes." You will then have a horrible aversion to rice of any kind for the rest of your life, and your children will never respect you. But I digress.)

7 threads saffron per person

½ cup dry white wine

1 piece boneless chicken thigh, per person, cut into thirds

salt and pepper, to taste

½ teaspoon sweet smoked paprika, per person

olive oil, enough to cover the bottom of the pan

¼ cup finely chopped sweet onion, per person (I recommend Walla Walla Sweets, when they are in season.)

1 garlic clove, per person and finely minced

⅓ cup Bomba rice, per person (Note: do not use another type of rice. If you don't use Bomba, you are a fool!)

1 ounce semi-soft chorizo, per person

¼ cup grated tomato, per person

3 clams, per person

2 large prawns, per person

garbanzo beans, already cooked

peas

lemon wedges and parsley, for garnish

Now that you have all your ingredients ready, it's time to start cooking. Step one, pour yourself some wine. Step two, roast the bell peppers. After roasting, peel off the skin and discard the seeds. Chop the roasted bell peppers into 3- by 1-centimeter pieces and set aside. In a heavy-bottomed pot, heat stock (not bouillon, remember) to a gentle simmer. Place the saffron in a saucepan on medium heat. Heat the saffron until it begins to become fragrant. Then toss in the wine. (When cooking with wine, the rule is if you wouldn't drink the wine, don't put it in your food!)

Pat chicken dry. Place in a large bowl and season with salt, pepper and half the paprika. Heat paella pan and add your olive oil. When the oil begins to smoke, add the chicken, browning both sides. Add the onion and sauté until it turns translucent. Stir in the garlic with the chicken and onion for about 15 seconds. Add the rice and chorizo. Stir the rice until every grain becomes coated with oil. This should take a few minutes.

Once the rice is coated, add the rest of the paprika and the grated tomato. Stir for another minute. Add the stock and saffron to the party. Do one final stir to scrape any bits stuck to the bottom of the pan and make the rice level.

This next part is very important: adjust the heat to a simmer and don't stir the pan. Disturbing the rice will make your paella sticky. That is fine if you want risotto—but we are making paella, so resist the urge.

When the pan is still soupy but you are starting to see grains of rice appear, you can add your clams. Once the rice has absorbed the stock, tuck the prawns into the rice. Next, spread the beans, roasted bell pepper and peas over the paella. When you begin to get a caramelized smell coming from the rice—not a burnt smell—the paella is finished. Remove the pan from the heat and cover with a wet towel for 5 to 10 minutes before serving. For garnishes, use lemon wedges and parsley.

Paella goes well with a variety of wines. I enjoy it with Tertulia Cellars Tempranillo or Tertulia Cellars "Redd Brand" Grenache.

Recipe courtesy of and authored by Ryan Raber, winemaker for Tertulia Cellars.

2014, Baron introduced his new label, "Horsepower." This new label was another limited wine with the first vintage release of 2011. It featured vineyards of Syrah, Grenache and Viognier planted very tightly, ranging from 3,555 to 4,840 vines per acre with as little as three- by three-foot spacing, planted one vine per stake, or *sur echalas* in French. One of the vineyards, in particular, follows the contour of what was once part of the old Walla Walla River.

The horse power behind the "Horsepower" are two Belgian draft horses. These broad, four-legged gentle work giants can maneuver between the vineyard rows using farming equipment that was created by a blacksmith in the Burgundy region of France and brought to the Walla Walla Valley. The practice is reminiscent of old nineteenth- and twentieth-century farming practices of Europe, which also made an appearance in the Walla Walla Valley when French settlers arrived.

In Walla Walla, the vintages of history are always repeating themselves.

7

THE VISIONARIES

It is not the critic who counts; not the man who points out how the strong man stumbles, or where the doer of deeds could have done them better. The credit belongs to the man who is actually in the arena, whose face is marred by dust and sweat and blood; who strives valiantly; who errs, who comes short again and again, because there is no effort without error and shortcoming; but who does actually strive to do the deeds; who knows great enthusiasms, the great devotions; who spends himself in a worthy cause; who at the best knows in the end the triumph of high achievement, and who at the worst, if he fails, at least fails while daring greatly, so that his place shall never be with those cold and timid souls who neither know victory nor defeat.
—*Theodore Roosevelt*

They drove around in an old pickup seeking land that would be suitable for planting grapes—wine grapes, in particular. Gary Figgins and Rick Small drove around Walla Walla County with the goal to be officially recognized as a wine destination, an American Viticultural Area (AVA).

An AVA is a wine grape–growing region in the United States that is distinguishable by its geographic features. Boundaries are defined by the Alcohol and Tobacco Tax and Trade Bureau (TTB) from the U.S. Department of the Treasury.

The Walla Walla AVA is a unique one, as it includes two state lines: 69 percent of the AVA is in Washington State, and the remainder is in Oregon. With the guidance of mother nature, the recognition is not about borders, but more about uniformity of climate, soil and elevation—or, as the French have so eloquently named it, terroir.

```
July 28, 1982


Director
Bureau of Alcohol, Tobacco and Firearms
Washington, D.C. 20226

Dear Sir:

Attached please find a petition for the establishment of the "Walla Walla Valley"
viticultural area, submitted in accordance with 27 CFR 4.25a(e)(2). The proposed
    cultural area includes lands in both Oregon and Washington States.

   is proposal was developed by the Walla Walla Valley Winegrowers Association,
   nich includes representatives from all existing vineyards and wineries in
the "Valley", potential growers and other interested persons.

We endeavored to state our case as briefly and succinctly as possible. However,
if additional information is required, we will be happy to provided it at
your request. Please address any questions to Darcey Fugman-Small at the address
below.

Thank you.

    erely,




   ichard L. Small
       ident, Walla Walla Valley Winegrowers Association
     J. Box  1533
Walla Walla, WA 99362



enclosures
```

The letter that started it all: the proposal for the Walla Walla Valley to become an American Viticultural Area. The letter is dated July 28, 1982, and signed by Rick Small of Woodward Canyon. *Courtesy of Darcey Fugman-Small, Woodward Canyon.*

The official federal designation for the Walla Walla Valley American Viticultural Area began in February 1984. However, when the AVA was designated, the TTB scaled down the proposed size from 300,000 acres to 260,000 due to only 60 of those acres being planted with wine grapes, such as Cabernet Sauvignon, Merlot, Syrah and Chardonnay. In 2001, the TTB approved the original boundaries of the Walla Walla Valley AVA.

Today, the Walla Walla Valley AVA is home to an average of 130 bonded wineries and over 1,800 acres of wine grapes, with additional acres of vineyards in the planning stages.

In 2014, the local winery and vineyard owners celebrated the thirtieth anniversary of the Walla Walla Valley AVA with honors from Washington,

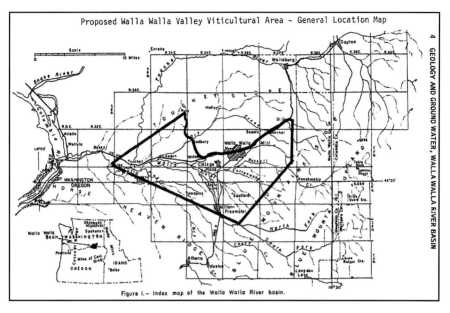

A map of the proposed Walla Walla Valley AVA. *Courtesy of the Walla Walla Valley Wine Alliance.*

D.C., where Representative Cathy McMorris Rodgers (WA-05), chair of the House Republican Conference, spoke on the House floor. Additionally, Senators Maria Cantwell (D-WA) and Patty Murray (D-WA) introduced a resolution on February 6, 2014, recognizing the anniversary and describing the Walla Walla Valley AVA.

In 2000, the Walla Walla Valley Wine Alliance (WWVWA) was formed. It is a nonprofit winery owner and grower membership organization whose primary mission is the marketing of the Walla Walla Valley wine region. It is the leading resource for visitors to the valley and other wine consumers. Every year, the WWWA chairs various events, such as Spring Release Weekend, Celebrate Walla Walla Valley Wine, Fall Release Weekend, Holiday Barrel Tasting and out-of-town tasting events in Seattle and Portland, Oregon.

THE SeVein Project

The beginning of a "fruitful" partnership was in 1997, when winery owners Gary Figgins, Norm McKibben and Marty Clubb and investor

Bob Rupar purchased the Seven Hills Vineyard. It was the start of the SeVein project—2,700 acres near Seven Hills that had been subdivided and would become the home to some of the most prestigious wine producers in the area, such as Amavi Cellars, Doubleback Winery, Figgins Family Wine Estates, L'Ecole No. 41, Pepper Bridge and a number of others. The group would also establish two companies to support property owners' development: North Slope Management and SeVein Water Association. SeVein Water Association gave each vineyard parcel water rights and a pro-rata share of the water association, which maintains the water system and public access roads.

One of the most recent celebrated parcels of the SeVein project is Ferguson Ridge, planted by Marty Clubb of L'Ecole No. 41, and named after his in-laws and founders of the winery, Baker and Jean Ferguson. In 2008, 9.6-acres of Cabernet Sauvignon, Merlot and Cabernet Franc were planted. The location of the parcel is at the 1,400-foot elevation south of Seven Hills Vineyard. A second-phase expansion was planted in 2009 with an additional 7.8 acres of Cabernet Sauvignon, Merlot and Syrah. This parcel was planted on top and just east of a 30-foot-tall exposed layer of fractured basalt.

The first vintage, with 845 cases produced, of the Ferguson Ridge estate was in 2011. Ferguson is a blend of 57 percent Cabernet Sauvignon, 32 percent Merlot, and 11 percent Cabernet Franc. The wine world was shocked, especially in the Northwest, when one of the largest and most prestigious wine competitions, Decanter World Wine Award, named the Ferguson as the best Bordeaux-style variety over fifteen pounds (twenty-five dollars) in the world. It was the only American wine to win an award in 2014.

The Marcus Whitman Hotel

In 1915, William McMurray, a passenger agent of the Oregon Railroad and Navigation Company, noted of Walla Walla: "One thing Walla Wallans should interest themselves in is the erection of a fine large modern hotel. Good hotels do much to advertise a city, also never fail to attract much travel. I would like to see Walla Walla with a hotel, second to none in the Northwest." In 1928, the early twentieth-century development in Walla Walla reached its highest point with the opening of the 174-room Marcus Whitman Hotel. W.W. Baker, president of Baker-Boyer National Bank, and more than two hundred other Walla Walla businessmen supported the idea of a luxury hotel to encourage tourism. A Seattle-based company, Real Estate Improvement Company, offered to invest $300,000 in the construction of a hotel, with the stipulation that the community raise $150,000 in ninety days—and it succeeded. The businessmen sold $100 shares of stock in just a few short weeks. Travelers, conventioneers, celebrities and even dignitaries, including President Dwight D. Eisenhower, would visit the grand downtown hotel, located on Second Avenue and Rose Street.

The Marcus Whitman Hotel is located on Second Avenue, Walla Walla. This image is from the 1930s. *Courtesy of Catie McIntyre Walker.*

Through the years the hotel saw many owners, and by the 1970s, fifty-some years later, the building became derelict, like 30 percent of the rest of downtown vacant space. A young entrepreneur, Kyle Mussman, developed a new company, appropriately named Real Estate Improvement Company, and in 1999, he purchased the tallest building in downtown Walla Walla. He would share his vision with the city and the port of Walla Walla. The timing was significant as in 1984, the Downtown Walla Walla Foundation was organized to address the concerns of the vacancy rate of the declining downtown. The foundation adopted the Main Street Four-Point Approach™ of revitalization, focusing on design, organization, promotion and economic restructuring.

The magnificent Marcus Whitman Hotel and Conference Center officially opened in the spring of 2001. Eventually, the third, fourth and fifth floors of the historic tower were renovated in 2007 from former office spaces to luxury guest rooms. Today, the hotel provides up-to-date technology for conference needs, an award-winning restaurant and a lounge featuring the best Walla Walla wines, and five individually owned winery tasting rooms are available off the hotel's grand lobby.

THE INSTITUTE OF ENOLOGY AND VITICULTURE

Dr. Myles J. Anderson is the founding director of the Institute of Enology and Viticulture at Walla Walla Community College as well as the owner-partner of Walla Walla Vintners. *Courtesy of Walla Walla Community College.*

If you are a lover of wine, the best college class to attend is one that teaches enology and viticulture. In 2000, there were over twenty wineries in the valley, and to keep the wine industry perpetuating, more people participating in it were needed. Dr. Myles J. Anderson, a thirty-one-year employee with Walla Walla Community College, served as counselor, instructor and administrator and eventually became the founding director for the Institute for Enology and Viticulture. In 2000, Anderson teamed up with WWCC president Steven VanAusdle to create hands-on programs in enology and viticulture.

Anderson, a distinguished winemaker in his own right, previously launched Walla Walla Vintners in 1995 with partner Gordy Venneri, the ninth winery to be bonded in the Walla Walla Valley. In January 2000, Anderson was charged with developing and launching the program. It would include obtaining an associate in applied arts and sciences degree in enology and viticulture (AAAS), viticulture science certificate or fermentation science certificate.

In 2002, joining Anderson to assist in developing the program was Stan Clarke. Clarke was a graduate of the U.S. Air Force Academy and held a bachelor of science degree in viticulture from the University of California–Davis and a master's degree in teaching from Washington State University. Clarke had previously served as grower relations manager at Ste. Michelle Wine Estates and had been a manager of various wineries and vineyards across the state. In 1987, he would serve as president of the Washington Wine Institute, the predecessor to the Washington Wine Commission.

Walla Walla Community College raised $5 million in private donations, and by 2003, the Center for Enology and Viticulture was up and running.

Stan N. Clarke is the former associate director of the Institute of Enology and Viticulture at Walla Walla Community College. *Courtesy of Walla Walla Community College.*

The building would include a state-of-the-art teaching commercial winery, the first in Washington State, named College Cellars, as well as a teaching kitchen for the Culinary Arts program, which supplied an associate in applied arts and sciences degree in culinary arts. Besides the center, the institute also developed its own teaching vineyards that were planted and maintained by the students.

On November 29, 2007, Stan Clarke passed away at his home in Walla Walla County, leaving a huge loss not only in the Walla Walla wine community but also across the state. In 2008, Stan Clarke was posthumously inducted into the Legends of Washington Wine Hall of Fame at the Walter Clore Wine and Culinary Center in Prosser, Washington. (Clore was the "Father of the Washington Wine Industry.")

In 2011, Dr. Myles J. Anderson was selected as an inductee to the Legends of Washington Wine Hall of Fame at the Clore Center. He retired his position as director in 2013 but continues on the advisory committee for the Institute for Enology and Viticulture.

Chocolate Bliss

Serves 8

15 ounces semi-sweet chocolate, diced

4 tablespoons unsalted butter

½ cup powdered sugar

1 cup heavy cream

4 egg yolks

6 tablespoons spirit of choice

Melt diced chocolate, butter, sugar and heavy cream over double boiler until mixture reaches 120 degrees. Remove from heat, fold in egg yolks and spirit.

Mold into desired shapes and allow to cool for 4 hours in refrigerator to set up.

Remove gently and slice or serve as formed.

Recommended wine pairing: College Cellars of Walla Walla Malbec or Late Harvest Wine.

Recipe courtesy of Chef Dan Thiessen, executive director/instructor of the Culinary Arts Program at Walla Walla Community College.

STE. MICHELLE WINE ESTATES

Chateau Ste. Michelle Winery, Washington State's founding winery, was formed in 1967. It has been influential on many of the projects and wineries in Walla Walla over the years. In the 1990s, Ste. Michelle Wine Estates recognized the importance of Merlot in Washington State. Because Washington lies on the same latitude as France's Bordeaux region, where Merlot is grown for blends, it makes sense for Washington to keep the same focus. Jancis Robinson, a British wine critic and journalist, summed up Washington's suitability for Merlot when she said, "I've always been impressed by Washington State merlot. It just sort of jumped out of the glass at me...You just feel this is right: this is not an attempt at something, this is something."

In 1994, Ste. Michelle Wine Estates released its first vintage of Merlot under the Northstar Winery label. A state-of-the-art winery, Northstar is located south of Walla Walla. In the early years of Northstar Winery, it was guided by celebrated California winemaker Jed Steele. David "Merf" Merfeld served as Northstar's assistant winemaker, and in 2005, Merfeld became the head winemaker. He holds a degree in horticulture with an emphasis in viticulture and enology from Washington State University.

THE WINE VILLAGE

In 2006, the Port of Walla Walla, with the assistance of a state economic stimulus grant, constructed three buildings to serve as space for new startup wineries, also known as "incubators." The project cost over $1 million and would be built at Piper Avenue, at the Port of Walla Walla by the Walla Walla Regional Airport. Once again, Walla Walla visionaries Dr. Myles Anderson and Norm McKibben were consulted on the production and layout of a winery.

The idea of the "wine village" was embraced by the wine community as well as tourists, and by 2008, two more buildings were constructed. Inside the five whimsical-colored buildings are winemakers with an entrepreneurial spirit and the dream of someday flying away from the incubators to be on their own. To be effective, each winery had the capacity to produce two thousand cases a year. In the beginning, these actual working wineries (not just tasting rooms) take on a reasonably low monthly rental lease that gradually increases as they progress in their business until the rent maxes out at the end of the six-year lease. At that point, it will be time for them to leave the nest. This lease hopefully provides each winery the opportunity to use most of its startup funds for other necessities such as grapes, crush equipment, tanks and barrels. For now, the five wineries share a crush pad, and even more important, they also share a sense of community.

The first two wineries to take root at the incubators were Adamant Cellars and Trio Vintners. Later to the community came Lodmell Cellars, and in 2008, when the last two buildings were completed, CAVU Cellars and Kontos Cellars joined the flock. In the mean time, Adamant Cellars, Cavu Cellars, Lodmell Cellars and Trio Vintners have successfully moved onto different facilities. To fill the empty spaces, Corvus Cellars, Palencia Winery and Walla Faces Wine moved into the village, as did the first brewer to be in the village, Burwood Brewing Company. The brewery has added a new twist to the wine village but also builds on Walla Walla's history of brewing back in the early 1900s.

LONG SHADOWS VINTNERS

In 2000, Allen Shoup, a wine pioneer in Washington State and former CEO of Chateau Ste. Michelle and its affiliated wineries for seventeen years, developed a wine project like no other and chose Walla Walla to be the home.

Long Shadows Vintners was a state-of-the-art winery with a collection of ultra-premium wines produced by a "dream team" of celebrated winemakers from all over the world: Randy Dunn of Dunn Vineyards in Napa, California; Michel Rolland, Pomerol (southwestern France), vintner and consultant to many of the world's famous wineries; Armin Diel, proprietor of the renowned Schlossgut Diel in Germany's Nahe Valley; father-and-son team Ambrogio and Giovanni Folonari, Tuscany's oldest and most prestigious wine families from the late 1700s; John Duval, winemaker for twenty-eight years for Australia's most celebrated wine, Penfolds Grange; and wine consultants from Napa Agustin Huneeus Sr. and Philippe Melka.

This collection included winemakers Shoup had met in his journeys during his years at Chateau Ste. Michelle. The winery, located on Frenchtown Road, gave each vintner the opportunity to produce his or her wines using the best of Washington State's grapes. Under the Long Shadows consortium and the direction of French-born Walla Walla winemaker Gilles Nicault, each winemaker became an owner-partner in his special single wine crafted to showcase the area.

In 2008, Shoup became managing partner of the Benches at Wallula Gap, a 650-acre vineyard in the Horse Heaven Hills AVA. Long Shadows has collected numerous awards, including recognition as *Food & Wine* magazine's "2007 Winery of the Year." In 2014, Allen Shoup was inducted in the Legends of Washington Wine Hall of Fame at the Walter Clore Wine and Culinary Center.

ARTIFEX WINE COMPANY

Once there were the ghosts in the sixteen-thousand-square-foot space originally assembled and constructed by local city fathers and grape juice magnets John G. Kelly and Donald Sherwood. The former Continental Can Company, and later Crown Cork and Seal building, came alive after being closed in 2002. The old Dell Avenue building had a history of former employees becoming a part of the new generation of Walla Walla winemakers.

In September 2007, the industrial building on Dell Avenue in Walla Walla became the home to Artifex Wine Company, eastern Washington's only dedicated custom crush facility. Here was another opportunity and a vision for Norm McKibben, who joined a new partnership with two other wine industry doyens, Rick Middleton and Jean-François Pellet. Middleton is the fourth generation of Anderson & Middleton Company in Hoquiam, Washington, owners of Cadaretta Wines in Walla Walla; Buried Cane Wines in Prosser, Washington; and Clayhouse Wines in Paso Robles, California.

Pellet, a third-generation Swiss-born winemaker, had produced wine not only in Switzerland but also in Germany and Spain. He arrived in California, and after four years at the prestigious Heitz Cellars in Napa Valley, he moved to Walla Walla, became the founding winemaker at Pepper Bridge Winery and joined founder Norm McKibben as a partner at Amavi Cellars.

The ultra-premium wine producer offers full-service winemaking, ranging from small boutique wineries to medium-sized brands of both red and white wines. Full service includes everything from receiving fruit from the vineyard to the bottling and packaging of the finished wines. The total capacity of the facility of the finished wines is thirty-six thousand cases.

NEW PROJECTS

The valley continues to grow with new wineries stepping onto the scene nearly every year, especially with plantings of new vineyards and extending already established vineyards.

Justin Wylie of Va Piano Vineyards, along with Farms for America, has undertaken a new project named Eritage Vineyards. The project involves initially planting 180 acres on the 386-acre plot that was acquired north of the Walla Walla Valley. Thirty international investors are contributing to the project, as part of the EB-5 Program, an economic program designated by U.S. Citizenship and Immigration Services (USCIS). It was passed by the U.S. Congress in 1990. The immigrant investors must invest $1 million in a new commercial enterprise that will not only benefit the U.S. economy but also create a minimum of ten full-time jobs. The first plantings of Cabernet Sauvignon, Merlot, Cabernet Franc, Malbec and Syrah took place in 2014.

On the North Fork of the Walla Walla River at 1,200 feet elevation are fifteen acres of planted vineyards that may never have to worry about frost. Tertulia Cellars, with Ryan Raber as head winemaker and Ryan Driver as vineyard manager, has developed an estate vineyard on the Oregon side of the Walla Walla Valley AVA. The total amount of planned vineyard is twenty-three acres with Cabernet Sauvignon, Merlot, Cabernet Franc, Malbec, Petit Verdot and Syrah to be planted, as well as white grapes of Marsanne and Roussanne. Most of the steep slope is terraced with two rows of vines placed on each ten-foot terrace. The vineyard faces south, which allows for the optimum sun to create ideal conditions for ripening fruit, and the soil consists of silt and fractured basalt.

When Christophe Baron discovered stones in the bed of the old Walla Walla River that reminded him of the those in the famed Châteauneuf-du-Pape wine region in France, the thought of "The Rocks District of Milton-Freewater" American Viticultural Area was probably not the first that came to his mind. However, in 2014 a newly proposed American Viticultural Area was submitted to the TTB. "The Rocks District of Milton-Freewater" will be a sub-appellation of the existing Walla Walla Valley AVA. The proposed area will encompass 3,767 acres, or 4.9 square miles. Dr. Kevin Pogue, geology professor at Whitman College–Walla Walla, submitted the proposal in February 2014. Pogue also owns and operates VinTerra, a vineyard site and terroir consulting and marketing company.

From the days of the local orchard pioneers such as A.B. Roberts and Dr. Nelson Blalock, the rocky area was known for its orchards and vineyards from the mid-1800s to the Depression era.

The proposed area includes four wineries and 250 acres of vineyards, and it is known for its Syrah and other southern red Rhône-style wines. The petition names nineteen wine producers that have vineyards within the proposed AVA. Four of the nineteen also have winery facilities within the proposed AVA. Those wineries include Beresan Winery, Buty Winery, Cayuse Vineyards, Charles Smith Wines, Delmas Wines, Don Carlo Vineyard, Dusted Valley Vintners, Figgins Family Wine Estates, Proper Wines, Otis Kenyon Wine, Rasa Vineyards, Reynvaan Family Vineyards, Riverhaven Cellars, Rôtie Cellars, Saviah Cellars, Sleight of Hand Cellars, Watermill Winery, Waters Winery and Zerba Cellars. At this time, the establishment for "The Rocks District of Milton-Freewater" AVA is in the current State of TTB Regulatory Timeline and waiting on the final ruling. Pogue expects "The Rocks District of Milton-Freewater" to be official in December 2014.

We wait and will continue to watch. Wine history is rich in the Walla Walla Valley, and its wines have made an indelible impression not only locally but also around the world.

Walla Walla made the pleasantest impression upon my mind of any city I visited while in the Northwest. Whenever I think of Walla Walla I can smell sweet perfume of the thousand locust trees which lined the streets and can see the radiant beauty of the city on that day in May when I was there. The glory of the spring air and sunshine together with the beauty of the city, made an indelible impression on my mind, and I will never forget the city.
—Theodore Roosevelt, 1903

AFTERWORD

The arrival of this book could not be timelier. As this book goes to press, Walla Walla is celebrating the thirtieth anniversary of the Walla Walla Valley American Viticulture Area (AVA). Indeed, there is much to reflect on and contemplate when one considers the history of the region and its settlement by European descendants to the contemporary history of the economic development of the local wine industry.

Not long after Lewis and Clark made their way to the mouth of the Columbia River, Walla Walla became the inland entrepôt of westward colonial expansion. However, as urban industrialization rooted in coastal regions, Walla Walla's position as a mercantile center was eclipsed by Seattle, Portland and Vancouver, British Columbia. From that point on, Walla Walla would remain a quintessential peripheral region, largely dependent on industries producing low-order commodities, such as agriculture, food processing and natural resource extraction. However, about thirty years ago, something interesting began to unfold that would inject dynamism into a stagnant local economy, diversify the economic base and increase the total regional output. While wheat and sweet onions continue to evoke imagery of the local economy, nowadays mentioning Walla Walla will suggest wine to the listener.

The roots of the contemporary wine industry trace back to 1977 with the establishment of Leonetti Cellar. However, until 1991 there were only 6 wineries in the valley, which is more like a handful of small businesses than what would be identified as an industry. Yet by 2000, there were 23 wineries, and by 2007, the number exceeded 90. Today, in the late spring of 2014, there are about 150 wineries in the Walla Walla Valley.

A similar pattern holds for vineyard acreage. When the AVA was established in 1984, there were about 65 acres dedicated to wine grapes; in 2006, the planted vineyard acreage amounted to more than 1,500, and today, there are upward of 2,500 acres either bearing fruit or prepared for planting, with new sites regularly identified and uncovered. This is formally illustrated by the 2014 petition to the Federal Alcohol and Tobacco Tax and Trade Bureau (TTB) to establish "The Rocks of Milton-Freewater AVA," which upon approval, will certify a sub-appellation nested within the Walla Walla Valley and the Columbia Valley AVAs. What began as a handful of wineries accompanied by a few dozen vineyard acres has evolved into a "cluster" or "complex" of economic activity driving ancillary growth in hospitality and tourism with enology and viticulture at its core.

As the volume of investment in the wine industry began to take off in the late 1990s, there was a sense that a labor shortage was on the horizon. In 2000, Walla Walla Community College (WWCC) established a degree program in enology and viticulture designed to prepare individuals for successful careers in the wine industry. After a few years, anecdotal evidence suggested economic change was unfolding at a rapid pace evinced by the establishment of new wineries, vineyard investments, sold-out hotel rooms and restaurants on wine weekends, increased tasting room sales and an increased volume of foot traffic in the newly redeveloped downtown. As such, there was keen interest to systematically analyze and report the wine industry's economic contribution to the regional economy.

As a graduate student at the University of Washington, I became aware of the recent and rapid growth of the industry, as well as the pioneering wine program launched by WWCC. I set out to conduct my dissertation research on the economic development of the Walla Walla wine cluster. At the same time, I was contracted by WWCC to lead a research team to study the regional economic impact of the wine industry. The *Economic Analysis of the Walla Walla Wine Cluster: Past, Present and Future* was published in July 2007. Our findings showed that the wine cluster could be credited with generating 2,169 jobs, resulting in total regional earnings of $103.2 million, and comprised 8.5 percent of the regional employment base.

A mere fourteen months after publishing our results, the United States was at the center of greatest economic contraction since the Great Depression. What did that mean for the Walla Walla wine industry and the regional economy in general? That was the question we sought to answer five years beyond completing our first study. We published *Revisiting the Economic Impacts of the Walla Walla Wine Cluster* in July 2011. To our surprise, the wine cluster and the regional economy were doing quite well, comparatively. Perhaps that is because Walla Walla was largely outside the (sub)urban housing bubbles that popped all over the country and is less reliant on non-earnings income and rents? Either way, the data showed a robust regional economy, demonstrating Walla Walla was an economic island of success in a dark sea of gloom and doom. Our findings demonstrated that the wine cluster had added 2,740 jobs since 2007, now totaling just over 6,000, while the U.S. economy experienced negative growth in employment. Total regional earnings more than doubled, from $103.2 million to $230 million, and comprised 14.4 percent of the region's employment base. Our work suggests the share of the wine economy will increase to about 20 percent of regional employment by 2020.

In a short time, the Walla Walla wine economy grew from a smattering of wineries you could list on one hand to a dynamic industry cluster that is constantly changing and difficult to track. At risk of stating the obvious, the dynamism underpinning the economic development of the wine cluster is driven by the production of high-quality wine and the global reputation of quality that was earned and maintained by the valley's pioneering wineries. When I was collecting data in 2007, I asked several people where they thought the industry was going. Those who had been around from the early days never imagined there would be 100 wineries in the valley, let alone 150 and climbing. Whether we see investments continue at an exponential pace or taper off, one thing remains certain—the Walla Walla wine industry will continue to generate a significant contribution to the Walla Walla regional economy, and that is something to appreciate, if not outright celebrate.

DR. NICHOLAS VELLUZZI
Director of Institutional Planning, Research and Assessment
Walla Walla Community College

BIBLIOGRAPHY

Carlson, Robert J., and Kevin R. Pogue. *Flood Basalts and Glacier Floods: Roadside Geology of Parts of Walla Walla, Franklin, Columbia Counties, Washington.* Olympia: Washington Division of Geology and Earth Resources, 1996.

Cayuse Vineyards. http://cayusevineyards.com.

Clore, Walter J., and Ronald Irvine. *The Wine Project: Washington State's Winemaking History.* Vashon, WA: Sketch Publications, 1997.

Frenchtown Historic Site. www.frenchtownpartners.org.

"History of Walla Walla." Walla Walla County Official County Government Site, 2012. http://www.co.walla-walla.wa.us/history.shtml.

Kershner, Jim. "Irrigation in the Walla Walla River Valley." November 14, 2013. Essay 10660, HistoryLink.org. http://www.historylink.org.

Locati, Joe J. "Agricultural History: The Walla Walla Sweet Onion and Its French Connection." *Pacific Northwest Forum* 3, nos. 2–3 (Spring–Summer 1978).

Lund, Jens. "Walla Walla Sweets: Onions and Ethnic Identity in a Pacific Northwest Italian Community." *Columbia Magazine,* Fall 1994.

Lyman, William Denison. *Lyman's History of Old Walla Walla County: Embracing Walla Walla.* Vol. 1. San Francisco, CA: W.H. Lever, 1852–1920.

McLeod, Sam. *Bottled Walla.* Walla Walla, WA: Detour Farm Publishing, LLC, 2005.

National Register of Historic Places Inventory. "Saturno-Breen Truck Garden." U.S. Department of the Interior Heritage Conservation and Recreation Service, January 4, 1982.

Okrent, Daniel. *Last Call: The Rise and Fall of Prohibition*. New York: Scribner, 2011.

Pogue, Kevin R. "Folds, Floods, and Fine Wine: Geologic Influences on the Terroir of the Columbia Basin." *Geological Society of America Field Guide* 15 (2009): 1–17.

Sherwood Trust. http://www.sherwoodtrust.org.

Smucker, Samuel. *The Life of Col. John Charles Fremont, His Narrative of Explorations and Adventures*. New York, Auburn: Miller, Orton & Mulligan, 1823–1863. https://archive.org/details/lifeofcoljohncha01fr.

Up to the Times magazine, vol. 2. Walla Walla Publishing Company, 1907. Reprinted as an e-book.

Walla Walla Union-Bulletin. "Pioneering Determination Is Seen in History of Attalia." February 24, 1946. http://newspaperarchive.com.

Weiser, Kathy. "Native American Legends: Walla Walla, People of Many Waters." Legends of America, August 2012. http://www.legendsofamerica.com/na-wallawalla.html.

Williams, Alice, comp. Italians in Walla Walla Collection, 1917–2011. Whitman College and Northwest Archives. http://nwda.orbiscascade.org/ark:/80444/xv66900.

INDEX

INDEX

ABOUT THE AUTHOR

Catie McIntyre Walker is a native of Walla Walla, Washington, and the original Walla Walla wine blogger, known as the Wild Walla Walla Wine Woman, since 2005. Over the past thrity-five years, as the wineries and vineyards grew in Washington State, her interest in this new industry, especially as it unfolded in Walla Walla, was piqued. She is a graduate of the Institute for Enology and Viticulture at Walla Walla and has been a wine judge for various wine competitions in the Northwest and a speaker and participant on panels regarding wine social media for writers and wineries. Catie is also a freelance writer and has written for *Walla Walla Lifestyles* magazine (*Walla*

Catie McIntyre Walker. *Photo taken by Courtney Mader.*

Walla Union-Bulletin), *Washington Tasting Room* magazine, *Northwest Palate* magazine (Portland, Oregon), *Palate Press: The Online Wine Magazine* and *Tourism Walla Walla.*